Layers

inspired collage
for paper projects with Meaning

shari carroll

NORTH LIGHT BOOKS
Cincinnati, Ohio
www.artistsnetwork.com

10 09 08 07 06   5 4 3 2 1

Distributed in Canada by Fraser Direct
100 Armstrong Avenue
Georgetown, ON, Canada L7G 5S4
Tel: (905) 877-4411

Distributed in the U.K. and Europe
by David & Charles
Brunel House, Newton Abbot, Devon,
TQ12 4PU, England
Tel: (+44) 1626 323200, Fax: (+44) 1626 323319
E-mail: mail@davidandcharles.co.uk

Distributed in Australia
by Capricorn Link
P.O. Box 704, S. Windsor,
NSW 2756 Australia
Tel: (02) 4577-3555

Library of Congress Cataloging-in-Publication Data

Carroll, Shari, 1959-
  Layers : inspired collage for paper projects with meaning / Shari Carroll.-- 1st edition.
     p. cm.
  Includes index.
  ISBN-13: 978-1-58180-784-4 (pbk. : alk. paper)
  ISBN-10: 1-58180-784-8 (pbk. : alk. paper)
  1. Photograph albums. 2. Scrapbooks. 3. Photocollage. I. Title.
TR501.C37 2006
  702.81'2--dc22

                        2006000419

metric conversion chart

TO CONVERT	TO	MULTIPLY BY
Inches	Centimeters	2.54
Centimeters	Inches	0.4
Feet	Centimeters	30.5
Centimeters	Feet	0.03
Yards	Meters	0.9
Meters	Yards	1.1
Sq. Inches	Sq. Centimeters	6.45
Sq. Centimeters	Sq. Inches	0.16
Sq. Feet	Sq. Meters	0.09
Sq. Meters	Sq. Feet	10.8
Sq. Yards	Sq. Meters	0.8
Sq. Meters	Sq. Yards	1.2
Pounds	Kilograms	0.45
Kilograms	Pounds	2.2
Ounces	Grams	28.3
Grams	Ounces	0.035

EDITOR: Jennifer Fellinger
COVER DESIGNER: Brian Roeth
INTERIOR DESIGNER: Amy Wilkin/Dragonfly
   Graphics, LLC
PRODUCTION COORDINATOR: Greg Nock
PHOTOGRAPHER: Christine Polomsky
PHOTO STYLIST: Nora Martini

F+W PUBLICATIONS, INC.

about the author

layer by layer

shari

DESIGNER MOTHER WIFE SISTER DAUGHTER FRIEND

DEDICATION

In the memory of
Jason
1985–2003
My student
My budding artist
My special boy

acknowledgments

I have had an incredible amount of support during the process of writing this book. First, I would like to thank my husband, Tom, and sons, Brooks and Scooter, for understanding my negligence in cooking dinners and doing laundry, and for putting up with the buried kitchen table and an extremely messy house. They encouraged me the whole way without complaints.

I would also like to thank my mother and sisters for always helping me grow as an artist. We all have an interest in one medium or another, and their enthusiasm is appreciated.

I could not have done this without the help and support from my friends at Hero Arts. My work with them has been my stepping stone to expanding my horizons as a project designer. They have allowed me to explore the boundaries of stamping.

I would like to thank my friends in the crafting industry who have supplied me with products and consistently boosted my confidence: Amy and Adrienne, Dana and Mary, Danny, Robin and Jennie, and Jennifer.

Christine Doyle, without you, this book would not have been possible; thank you for asking. I also wish to express my gratitude to my editor, Jenny Fellinger, and my photographer, Christine Polomsky, for holding my hand and guiding me through this unknown territory.

table of
contents

Lots of Layers 7 • Materials and Tools 8 • Techniques 12
Introduction to Projects 16

PROJECTS

from the heart:
Celebrating Love and Life 18

Sentimental Swatch Book 20
Love-in-the-Round Cards 22
Chalkboard Greetings 26
Love Coaster Set 30
Cherished Memories Book 34

childhood moments:
Capturing Memories of
Growing Up 38

Babyface Frame 40
Unfolding Story Tag 44
Teenage Canvas 48
"How to Raise a Red Head" Book 52
Maternal Memories Box 56

relationships
that inspire:
Treasuring Family &
Friends 62

"Niece of Mine" Memory Page 64
Clip-It Photo Frame 68
Clearly Friendship Card 72
Electrical Outlet Plate Frame 76
"My Three Men" Book 80

days gone by:
Documenting the Past 86

Vintage Image Bracelet 88
Library Pocket Card 90
Little Book of Inspiration 94
"T for Two" Memory Page 98
Screen Panel Book 102

carpe diem:
Seizing the Day 106

Miniature Daily Journal 108
Remember-to-Laugh Booklet 110
Bound Quote Collection 114
Collective Thoughts Journal 118
Celebration Wine Box 122

Resources 126
Index 127

from

the

first

moment

I saw

you

I

knew

It was

LOVE

MOM

SWEET

niece of mine

childhood

Encourage water sports

Play   Discover   curiosity

Bucket, hose and sunscreen not included

BOY

OOOOH

BOY

Laugh

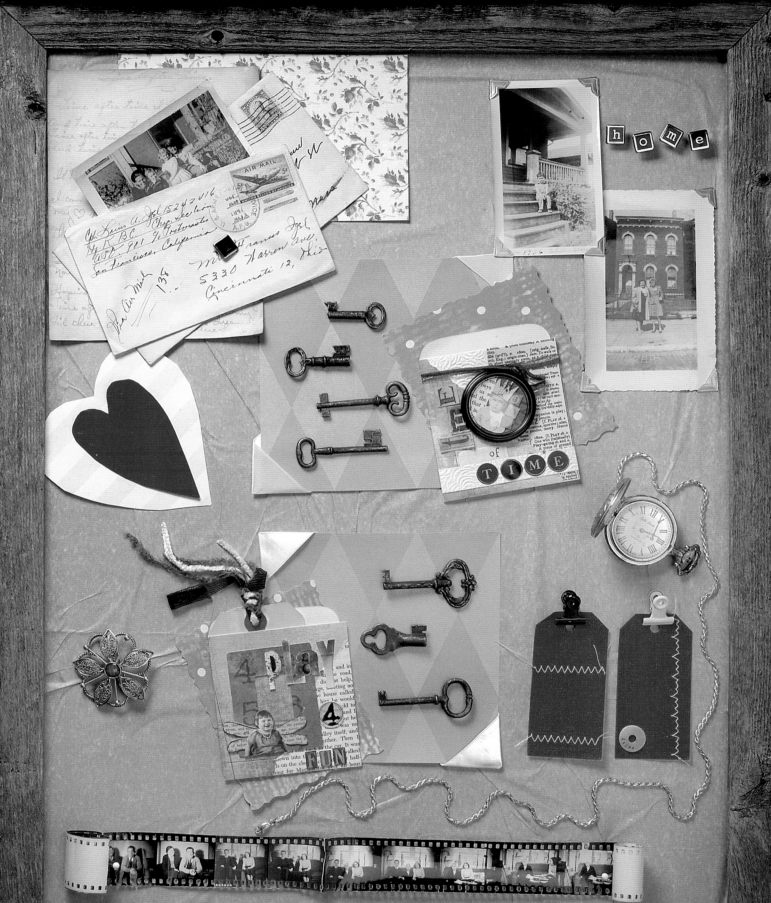

lots of layers

I once was asked what my work said about me, and I immediated replied, "Simple, with many layers." Though my response was off-the-cuff, I realized that I could not have said it any better had I taken a long time to consider my answer. It's in the way that I dress, the way that I think, and the way that I see the world. So, the straightforward title, *Layers*, is perfect for this book.

I am not complicated once the layers are revealed, nor is my work. To me, layering is simply a process of discovering the possibilities of combinations, a little like finding a combination of friends with personalities that just click. My projects click when I am able to successfully engineer the layers, balancing color, blending opposites, harmonizing light and dark, marrying word with image and text with pattern. A quirky way to think of layers is to imagine a dinner party: Consider the mixture of conversation, the merging of personalities, even the diversity of clothing. When it all works together, it can be quite a show!

The projects in this book are made up of many layers—in more ways than one. To begin with, the projects are collage-based, requiring a grad-ual buildup of paper and embellishment, color and pattern, texture and fiber. But beyond the physical layering of my work, there are tiers of meaning. I love to incorporate combinations of symbols, memories and feelings into my work—sometimes hidden, sometimes obvious, sometimes planned, sometimes spontaneous.

I will give you an example: Although my favorite number is eight, my designs usually reflect the number three. The reasons? It could be that I am one of three sisters, I am the third child, and I have three important men in my life. Or, perhaps it is something more spiritually-driven, like the trinity. There's also the sequence of yesterday, today and tomorrow, and the cycle of life, death and rebirth. One my favorite Celtic symbols is the triknot, a sign for motherhood. And, I am entering the third season of my life (as a writer!) and the third cycle as a woman. Whether the reasons are conscious or not, I always insert several aspects of myself into my art.

I hope that this book will help you discover the layers within your own life. Build your projects using emotions and memories as much as you use materials and techniques. Who knows? The result may be "Simple, with many layers."

materials and tools

To make the projects in this book, you will want to keep a few basic materials and tools handy at your work space. I have listed my personal "must haves" on the following pages. After trying many different crafting products, supplies and gadgets, I have formed opinions about what works the best and what looks the best. But your opinion is important, too! Feel free to experiment and find out what your favorites are.

paper

As you can imagine, paper is the most essential element in projects that involve layering. I love paper! With all the choices available, it is difficult to decide on just a few, so I don't—I just get everything that I like! I do use different types of papers for various purposes, depending on their texture, weight or look. I have compiled a list of what I typically use, which may help with your own selections.

Cardstock is a heavyweight paper used in scrapbooking and cardmaking. It comes in a variety of colors, patterns, textures and weights. I use cardstock as a backing for many of my projects and as the base for my scrapbook pages.

Printed paper, also referred to as **decorative paper** in this book, is an average- to lightweight paper primarily used in scrapbooking, though it is now a popular choice for cardmaking. It is available in a plethora of colors, patterns, scripts, florals and themes. This is my absolute favorite paper to work with.

Vellum is a lightweight, translucent film that lends itself well to layering with other papers. Vellum, which is available in solid colors, beautiful prints and embossed textures, accepts permanent inks and is suitable for stamping.

Acetate is a clear film that can be used with rubber stamps and permanent solvent-based inks. I use it to create clear cards and to add stamped messages over other artwork.

An **ink-jet transparency** is a clear film that can be used for computer-generated text and images. I use it when printing photographs and other typewritten effects to create a personalized transparency.

Chipboard is a thick, durable compressed paper, usually a brown or gray color. Somewhat like cardboard but thinner, chip-board is great for making small boxes and other paper crafts. I often use it in the construction of projects because it is sturdy yet can be cut with scissors.

adhesives

When creating layered projects, adhering materials to one another is essential. For this reason, adhesives are critical for many of these projects. There are several types of adhesives, each serving an important function.

Glue sticks are most appropriate for layering paper onto paper. Because of the glue stick's lack of water, it does not warp papers as liquid glue does. It also works well when adhering lightweight cloth to paper. I use a glue stick in all of my collage work, especially when gluing torn papers in place.

Tacky glue works well for adhering paper to plastic and decorative trim to projects. While tacky glue is much thicker than average white glue, its drying time is faster. My tacky glue of choice is Aleene's.

Découpage medium, or découpage glue, is especially effective for gluing paper to canvas. It provides a durable final coat for projects such as boxes, which

Paper and Adhesives: cardstock, patterned vellum, acetate, glue stick, découpage medium, double-sided tape, adhesive dots (Glue Dots), printed decorative paper

have a hard backing. When applying découpage medium to a surface, use an applicator brush for even coverage.

Double-sided tape, available in permanent and repositionable varieties, is excellent for mounting papers together. You can buy this kind of tape in easy-to-use roll dispensers.

Adhesive dots are double-sided, pressure-sensitive adhesive stickers. They come in roll form, and are available in a range of sizes, thicknesses and tack levels. Adhesive dots are best for sticking heavier items, such as buttons, flowers and metal objects, to paper projects. In the same category, **foam dots** are double-sided, adhesive dots with foam in the center. These dots, which raise objects off the paper, are perfect for adding dimension to your projects. You can also get foam adhesives in tape form, squares and it comes in an array of thicknesses.

the fun stuff: stamps, embellishments and decorative supplies

Oh, how I love to add texture, doodads and finishing touches to my layered projects! I cannot possibly name all the embellishments I use, so I will just mention my favorites. It is up to you to choose your preferred picks.

Stamping supplies are a basic component of my crafting supply stash. **Rubber stamps**, which come unmounted or mounted on wood or clear acrylic, are used with ink to add images, words or letters to project surfaces. Your selection of ink is broad. **Dye ink** is a quick-drying, water-based ink that yields the best results on paper. It is not recommended for embossing. **Pigment ink** is a thick, slow-drying water-based ink. It is recommended for embossing on paper. **Solvent ink** is a permanent, water-resistant ink. It can be used on paper and fabric as well as plastics, acetate, metals, glass and other slick surfaces. There are numerous specialty inks on the market, including chalk inks, watermark inks and distress-staining inks.

It is worth experimenting with all the possibilities to find your favorite effects!

Paints and stains are liquids used for adding color to paper. I use white acrylic paint, coffee and walnut stains to distress paper, applying each directly onto the surface with a makeup sponge (see page 13 for more information).

Tags, stickers and **ephemera** are items that can be used to embellish any project. For new and exciting looks, they can be altered in many different ways— sanded, stamped on, written on, distressed with inks, and more. With these versatile materials, anything goes.

Office supplies, such as staples, tabs and labels, can give a project a distinctive look. For a vintage touch, I like incorporating old, outdated office supplies, such as library pockets and sales tags, into my artwork.

Ribbons and **sewing notions** are popular embellishments that can be used in so many ways. I find inspiration in pretty laces, silk ribbon, woven trim, fabric swatches, knitting yarn, straight pins, hat pins, safety pins and snaps. Visit a fabric store to see what kinds of charming elements you can dig up.

Eyelets, brads and **studs** provide fancy ways of holding layers of papers together. These embellishments are found in a wide range of colors, sizes and shapes. Eyelets must be attached with a setter, while brads and studs have prongs that pierce and attach to paper.

Miscellaneous scrapbooking supplies come in all forms. There are flowers made of silk and paper; miniature decorative metal frames; doorknobs and bookknobs; metal charms featuring a variety of decorative words, messages, shapes and colors ... the list goes on and on. Let yourself be inspired by the variety!

cutting, piercing and punching tools

You will need sharp tools for cutting, piercing and punching paper, which are some of the fundamental techniques for creating successful layered projects.

Scissors, especially a sharp, high-quality pair, are a must. Keep this pair for cutting paper and cloth only, and keep another inexpensive pair for other jobs that may dull the blades, such as cutting cardboard or plastic.

Craft knives are used for trimming areas that scissors cannot reach. Be sure to always work with sharp blades.

Paper trimmers come in rotary, sliding and guillotine varieties.

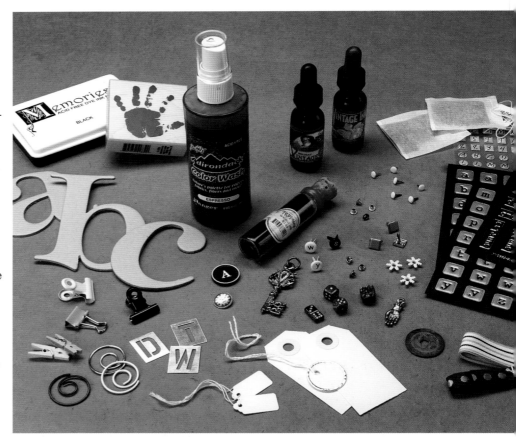

"The Fun Stuff" clockwise from left: inkpad and rubber stamp, walnut inks, tea bags, letter stickers, decorative ribbon, brads and eyelets, charms, tags, letter stencils, assorted clips, chipboard letters

Sliding paper trimmers often come with a handy attachment for scoring.

Awls are used for piercing paper. I use awls to pre-pierce small holes when attaching buttons to heavy surfaces.

A **Japanese screw punch** is a hole-punching tool that can be used anywhere on a sheet of paper without the need for a hammer. This must-have device comes with a selection of changeable attachment blades for creating holes of different sizes. The punch screws itself into the paper and is capable of penetrating through many layers. When I purchased my screw punch, I put away all my other hole punches—and I haven't looked back since!

An **eyelet setter** and **hammer** are used to set eyelets into paper. There are now screw-type eyelet setters available, which work like a Japanese screw punch, with no need for a hammer.

A **self-healing cutting mat** protects your work surface from damage that could be caused by craft knives, awls, screw punches and eyelet setters. Because it provides such a versatile and practical surface, I

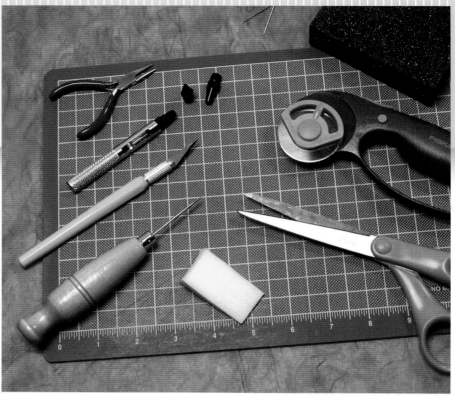

Tools clockwise from top, left: needle-nose pliers, hole punch exchangable tips, sanding block, rotary cutter, scissors, makeup sponge, awl, craft knife, hole punch, self-healing cutting mat

have included a cutting mat on the Materials and Tools list for every project in this book.

miscellaneous tools

There are some random tools that every crafter should keep accessible. You may not use these for every project, but they sure come in handy in a pinch!

A **scoring tool**, such as a bone folder, is used to score and crease paper. Some slide trimmers also come with a scoring attachment.

A **sanding block** is a firm, foam block lined with sandpaper. Sanding blocks are marketed as home improvement tools, but I use them all the time for distressing the edges of my projects. If you do not have a

sanding block, a piece of regular sandpaper will do.

Needle-nose pliers can be used for fine-detail work, such as removing button shanks and bending jump rings and wire.

Makeup sponges are ideal for applying dyes, stains and inks to paper and to rubber stamps. These dense, white wedges are inexpensive and disposable.

Sewing machine and/or sewing needles make it possible to add decorative or functional stitching to projects. Some machines have fancy stitch options, though I prefer the basic zigzag- and straight-stitching.

techniques

Knowing how to use your tools and supplies is an important factor in the outcome of your project. If you are uncomfortable with any technique or if you are not getting the results you intended, don't fret. With practice and experimentation, you will soon be achieving your goals. On the following pages, I have described the basic techniques that I use most often for the projects in this book. You can use my examples as a guide to get you started.

cutting paper

Cutting paper may sound like the most basic of techniques, but it shouldn't be overlooked. Getting the right cut will give you a better project. It is important to use the right tool for the job. And, whether cutting with scissors or using a trimmer, your equipment should always be in good working order with clean, sharp blades.

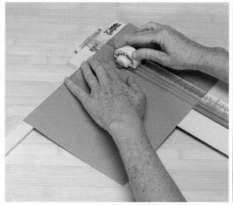

Cut with paper trimmer. A sliding paper trimmer, which has measured markings, is the ideal tool for cutting paper to a specific size. Most trimmers feature a straightedge guide at the top so you can trim your edges square.

Cut with scissors. Items that have a straight line guide can be easily cut by hand with scissors. For example, in the image above, the edge of the paper-covered book cover provides a guide for cutting away the excess paper. Scissors are also my choice when cutting out flowers, ribbon and other embellishments.

Cut with craft knife. Craft knives are perfect tools for cutting out difficult areas, such as tiny holes or frame windows. The sharp point of the blade fits into tight corners without causing any overcuts. When working with a craft knife, I always place the project on a self-healing cutting mat before cutting it.

As paper ages, it naturally tends to turn yellow or pale brown. This aged look has become a very desirable effect in scrapbooking and other paper arts. When you are distressing white or cream paper with ink, it makes sense to use a brown, ochre or yellow inkpad. One of my favorite products for this purpose is Ranger's Distress Ink. If you are aging paper of other colors, consider using pale tones of blues, pinks and greens. For an interesting effect, try mixing coordinating colors. When staining and dying items, always create a few extras just in case you make any mistakes later. Keeping a few extras on hand is also helpful in streamlining the creation of multiple projects.

distressing surfaces

A distressed appearance is one of my favorite looks. One reason is that it eliminates the pressure of perfectionism; when you are working with a style that embraces imperfection, there's no need to be precise and faultless. Because most of the paper, fabric and other project surfaces I buy are brand new, I often need to "wear them down" a bit before I incorporate them into my projects. To achieve a time-worn or weathered appearance, I distress surfaces in one of a few different ways.

Sand surface. Using a sanding block or piece of sandpaper, sand the edges of the surface. Allow the sandpaper to remove some of the top layer to create a worn look. Before beginning, determine what parts of the project would get the most wear and tear, then sand these areas with more vigor. Because it has firm edges, a sanding block is ideal for creating scratches and deep creases.

Stain surface with coffee or tea solution. Create a solution with hot water and either instant coffee granules or a tea bag. Apply the (cooled) solution to the project surface, either by brushing the solution onto the project, dipping the project into the solution or using a cosmetic sponge. Uneven dying creates a more convincing aged effect. When finished, let the surface dry completely.

Rub surface over inkpad. Rub the entire surface of the project directly over the surface of an inkpad, giving the project a yellowed or stained appearance (see Tip, above).

Rub inkpad over project edges. Rub the inkpad directly over the edges of the project surface, allowing the rest of the surface to remain unstained.

stamping

Stamping is an ideal way to add layers of images onto one surface. Rubber stamps can be used with ink, paints and stains. (Refer to page 9 for more information on the varieties of inks.) There are different ways of inking a stamp, but I usually do so either by pressing the stamp onto an inkpad or by applying paint or stain to the stamp surface with a makeup sponge. It is always a good idea to practice stamping on scrap paper first to see how the design looks.

Use stamp with changeable bands. A stamp with changeable bands features letter dials, which can be turned to spell different words. After you have "dialed" the word of your choice, ink the stamp. Holding the handle or base steady, press the stamp onto the project surface, and release.

Use mounted stamps. Rubber stamps are most commonly mounted on wood. In most cases, the rubber is cut close to the stamp design so positioning is not a problem. Mounted stamps are user-friendly and ready to go. Just ink the stamp with the desired color of ink, paint or stain. Place the inked stamp over the surface, then press firmly and evenly, without rocking the stamp. Release the stamp.

Use acrylic stamps. Acrylic stamps are sticky and transparent. To use them, first arrange the individual stamps onto a clear acrylic block; the stamps' self-adhesive backing will keep them stable. If you are using individual letter stamps to spell a word, remember that the word must be spelled backward, as the stamp design will print in reverse. Tap an inkpad evenly onto the stamp, then press the inked stamp onto the project surface, and release.

Use homemade stamps. You can make your own stamp with flexible craft foam. (The nice thing about handmade stamps is that they can be constructed to fit the exact size of the project.) Use a craft knife to cut the design from a piece of craft foam, then mount it onto a wood block with glue. Ink and stamp as you would with any other mounted stamp.

punching holes and setting eyelets

Hole-punching is an important technique to master if you plan to use eyelets, brads and other embellishments in your artwork. Using a Japanese screw punch, you can place holes anywhere on your page—plus you can punch through several layers of paper with ease. To set eyelets into a punched hole, follow these simple directions.

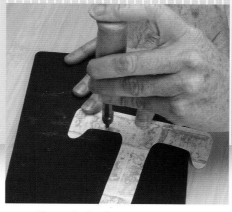

ONE. Punch hole. Place your project paper on a self-healing cutting mat. Determine where on the paper the hole needs to be placed, and position the screw punch accordingly. Hold the tool firmly in a vertical position, 90° to the paper, and press straight down. To penetrate thicker items or several layers of paper, a few pushes may be needed.

TWO. Place eyelet. Insert an eyelet into the hole, from the front.

THREE. Position eyelet setter. With the eyelet in place, flip the paper over so that it is face down on the cutting mat. Position the eyelet setter directly on top of the eyelet.

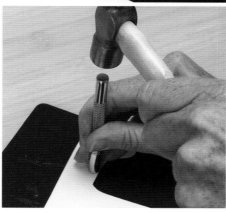

FOUR. Set eyelet. Once the eyelet setter is in place, hold it upright at a 90° angle to the paper. Tap the top end of the setter with a hammer to set the eyelet.

FIVE. Hammer eyelet. After the eyelet has been set, remove the eyelet setter. Gently tap on the back of the eyelet with a hammer.

the
projects

This book is divided into five inspirational sections, each dedicated to one significant aspect of life. The first section celebrates love; the second, childhood memories; the third, family and friends; the fourth, days gone by; and the last, the spirit of **carpe diem**. In each section, you will find a wide range of projects: books, cards, frames, journals, boxes, jewelry and more. They all capture the joys of my life, and I hope they will pass joy on to you, too. Because these projects will be made by your hands, they will become unique treasures the minute you add the finishing touch.

On the following pages, I will walk you step-by-step through each project. You will see how I assemble them from start to finish, layer by layer. I will also share with you the feelings, experiences and memories that originally motivated me to make the projects. In a sense, I am peeling back the layers of meaning, hoping to spark your imagination.

Remember, you can create your own layers. I have intentionally kept my directions general, allowing you to choose which papers and embellishments to use and how to use them. In many cases, I have listed the specific products that I worked with. That way, you can replicate the project exactly, if you wish. But feel free to use my projects as a starting point—because it's all about the layers you want **to create.**

from the heart:

celebrating love and life

love is such a splendid thing. The way I see it, there **is** truth to the expression "Love makes the world go 'round." We are all able to experience life's many layers of love by communicating this powerful emotion in different forms. A mother's unconditional love for her children creates a lifelong bond. Girlfriends share a connection so strong, they consider themselves sisters. Siblings, though they may not always show their love outwardly, have a special kinship. And then, of course, there is romantic love, the attraction of two beings that creates an unbreakable union.

With a great system of friends and family, I have been very fortunate to have experienced love on many different levels. My sisters and parents have been treasures in my life, and my children are a constant source of joy. I have also been extremely blessed with a wonderful husband of twenty years, who still surprises me with outward expressions of love and romance.

This first section explores ways of showing love through creativity. There are many things you can do to create thoughtful gifts from the heart: crafting a book to capture loving gestures, making a journal to preserve the romance in a marriage, fashioning interactive cards to say "I love you." These are all items that are sure to be cherished for years to come. So, take a little extra time and thought, and celebrate the important people in your life with these artful expressions of love.

sentimental
swatch book

My husband is a hopeless romantic. Since our courtship, he has always found ways to let me know that he is thinking of me. One of my favorite examples of his warm, creative and romantic spirit is the rock collection that he started for me years ago, and continues to build to this day. He works in construction and has a remarkable eye for finding rocks smaller than the size of a dime. So, he picks out unique rocks to add to my collection. What makes this collection so sentimental? Each rock that he selects is in the shape of a heart! This ongoing gesture of love is known only by the people who visit our home. I thought it would be fun to make a swatch book to pay tribute to this special expression of romance.

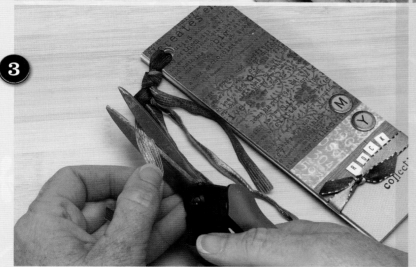

ONE. Disassemble book.
Disassemble the swatch book to separate the front cover, interior pages and back cover.

TWO. Apply paper to covers.
Use a glue stick to adhere decorative paper to the front cover. Add a few strips of coordinating decorative paper at the bottom. Trim off any excess paper along each edge of the cover. Apply decorative paper to the back cover in the same manner. Find the hole in the upper left corner of each cover, and using a craft knife, poke a hole through the decorative paper.

THREE. Embellish pages and reassemble book. Add stamps, stickers, rub-on letters and ribbons of your choice to the front cover. Reassemble the swatch book, but instead of reinserting the corner screw to keep the pages together, run a few decorative ribbons through the hole and tie in a knot to secure. Trim the ribbon ends. Add photos, images, text and other embellishments to the interior pages, as desired.

MATERIALS

swatch book (7 Gypsies)

decorative paper
* script design (7 Gypsies)
* yellow (Daisy D's)
* mustard numbers (Creative Imaginations)

favorite photograph(s)

rubber stamps
* letters (Hero Arts)
* additional designs of your choice, as desired

ink (Tsukineko StazOn Black)

embellishments
* letter stickers (EK Success)
* rub-on letters (Autumn Leaves)
* ribbon (May Arts, Yarn Fibers)
* additional embellishments of your choice, as desired

paper trimmer

craft knife

scissors

glue stick

self-healing cutting mat

love-in-the-round
cards

the circle is an endless line that represents eternity, which is why the wedding ring is such a perfect symbol of everlasting love and devotion in a marriage. I enjoy incorporating hidden symbolism into my work, including subtle signs, like the circle, that are simple but rich with meaning. So, I was excited when I came up with the idea of making circular love-themed cards. The significance of the card's shape may not be immediately obvious to the recipient, but that just makes the card even more special when it is understood "in the round." These charming collaged cards are the perfect size to be either displayed or tucked away in a journal.

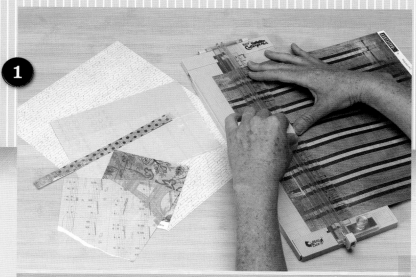

1

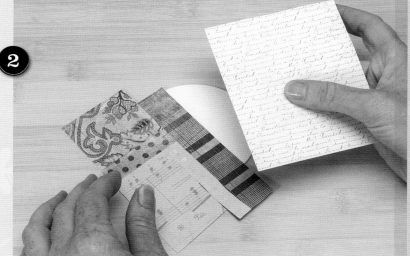

2

ONE. Cut decorative paper.
Use a paper trimmer to cut sheets of decorative paper into various sizes of squares and rectangles.

TWO. Cover coaster with paper.
Adhere the decorative paper to one cardboard disc with a glue stick, layering and overlapping the paper.

MATERIALS

three chipboard discs (River City Rubber Works)

decorative paper
* script (Autumn Leaves)
* music (Me And My Big Ideas)
* other prints (Basic Grey)

rubber stamps
* heart (Hero Arts)
* additional designs of your choice, as desired
* word stamp with changeable bands (JustRite Title Stamper)

ink (Ranger Distress Inks)

embellishments
* dry cleaner tag
* game letter tiles (EK Success)
* decorative button
* additional embellishments of your choice, as desired

waxed linen thread

paper trimmer

scissors

Japanese screw punch

glue stick

adhesive dots

sanding block

self-healing cutting mat

3

4

5

THREE. Trim paper. With scissors, trim the excess paper along the perimeter of the disc.

FOUR. Distress edges. Use a sanding block to distress the edges of the disc.

FIVE. Add stamps. Using a word stamp that has changeable bands, stamp the word "LOVE" along one of the decorative paper edges.

SIX. Make embellishment. Make a simple embellishment by stamping a heart (or other desired design) onto a dry cleaner tag or small piece of paper.

SEVEN. Punch hole. Use adhesive dots to stick the embellishment to the disc as desired. Punch a hole in the lower half of disc; this hole will be used to hold the "O" button embellishment in step 9.

6

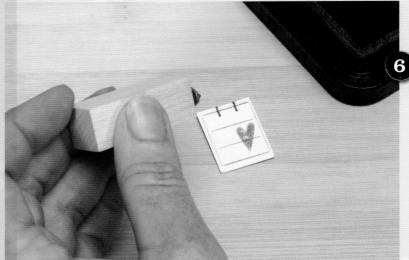

7

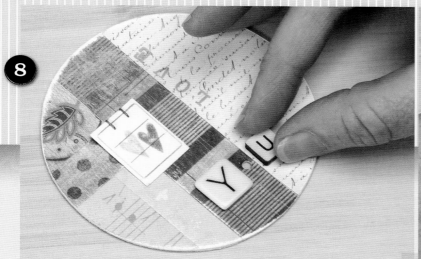

EIGHT. Add game letter tiles.
Using adhesive dots, stick two game letter tiles, *Y* and *U*, to the disc. Place *Y* to the left of the hole made in step 7, and place *U* to the right of it, as shown.

NINE. Add button. Run a length of waxed linen thread through the shank of a decorative button. Run the two ends of the thread through the hole made in step 7, then pull the thread tight and tie the two ends together to secure the button in place. (If the button doesn't have a shank, you can just glue it in place.)

TEN. Complete coaster set. Make two more love-themed discs to match the style of the first, using similar color palettes, coordinating paper and embellishments.

layers
of possibilities

When making a card, consider the recipient, and then go from there. How would you describe his or her personality? Inject some of that personality into the card! With my niece in mind, I used the cheerful colors of spring to come up with this variation, a fresh door hanging. To make it, cover the discs as you did in the main project, but this time adorn each with a letter to form the word "LOVE." Punch holes in the top and bottom of each piece, then connect them with ribbon or fiber.

chalkboard
greetings

My husband and I have the most unusual interactive message board system in our home. In the mornings, when the bathroom is filled with steam and I'm hastily getting ready for the day, I write a short love note to him on the mirror! He does the same for me after reading my "mirror message." The fun part about this ritual is that the words are invisible until the bathroom is steamy again, so the next message is always a surprise. This odd communication habit prompted me to make an interesting and equally interactive card that could be written, read and easily erased. Someday soon, I will leave this one by the coffeepot for my husband's morning note.

1

2

ONE. Spray chipboard. Cover the surface of a piece of chipboard with an even coat of spray-on chalkboard paint. Allow the paint to dry.

TWO. Cover frame. Using a glue stick, cover the front surface of a large slide mount frame with decorative paper. Trim any excess paper along the edges of the frame, then use a craft knife to trim out the interior window.

MATERIALS

chipboard

large slide mount frame
(Design Originals)

decorative paper
✳ rulers (Design Originals)

rubber stamps
✳ letters (Hero Arts)

ink (Tsukineko Staz-On Black)

spray-on chalkboard paint
(Krylon Chalkboard)

embellishments
✳ miniature paper tag
✳ scrapbook letter embellishments
   (Daisy D's Elements)
✳ game letter stickers
✳ decorative brads (Making Memories)
✳ ribbon
✳ additional embellishments of your
   choice, as desired

chalk

string

small metal clip
(Design Originals)

metal washer

craft knife

scissors

Japanese screw punch

glue stick

double-sided tape

self-healing cutting mat

③

④

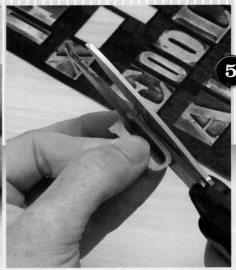

⑤

THREE. Cut chipboard. Cut the chalk-board-coated chipboard to the same outer dimensions of the frame.

FOUR. Make tag embellishment. Decide what message you want to include on the chalkboard frame. I decided to put "Did you know," which could then be followed by an erasable message in chalk. Once you have decided, stamp a miniature paper tag with the first word of your message.

FIVE. Make letter embellish-ment. Cut out scrapbook letter embellish-ments for the next word.

SIX. Create additional word embellishments. Make your final word embellishment(s) for the frame. For the word "know," I applied game letter stickers to a small scrap of coated chipboard, then mount-ed the board on a piece of decorative paper.

SEVEN. Assemble frame. Use dou-ble-sided tape to adhere the paper frame over the chalkboard-chipboard. Adhere the text embellishments along the top of the frame with a glue stick or double-sided tape. When you are satisfied with the design, use a screw punch to punch four holes in the frame: two in the upper left corner and one in each lower corner, as shown.

⑥

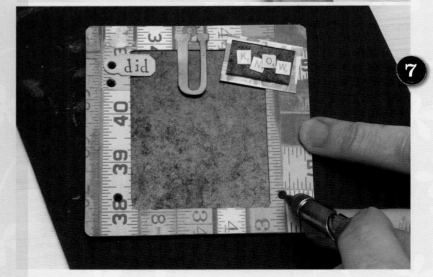

⑦

(8)

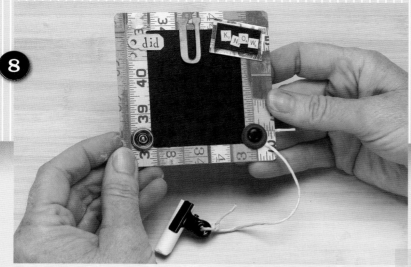

(9)

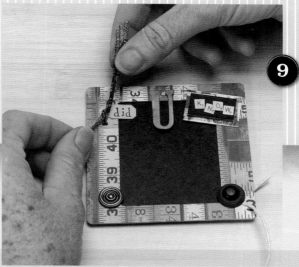

(10)

EIGHT. **Secure chalkboard clip to frame.** Place a decorative brad in the hole punched in the lower left corner. Attach a small metal clip to a length of string, securing the clip with a knot. Place a small piece of chalk in the clip. Then, run the string through the lower right hole, pulling about 1" (3cm) through to the other side. Position a washer over the hole in the lower right corner, placing it right over the cord. Run the prongs of another decorative brad through the hole, then bend the prongs to secure the brad in place; the brad will rest right on top of the washer, keeping it in place.

NINE. **Add ribbon.** Run a length of decorative ribbon through the two holes in the upper left corner so that both ends of the ribbon can be tied in front. Thread the stamped tag over one of the ends, then tie the ribbon in a knot to secure the tag.

TEN. **Write message.** Write the message of your choice on the framed chalkboard, using the chalk attached with the clip. When you want to change the text, you can easily erase the chalk with your fingers and write a new message.

layers of possibilities

Could there be a project any more appropriate for friends in the teaching profession? Show appreciation to the teachers you know with the chalkboard card or this variation, made with a sheet of acetate. Like the chalkboard surface, the acetate film can be written on with a dry-erase pen and easily wiped clean. For this variation project, cover a paper frame, as you did in the main project. Then, add a button, bow and key hole, using brads to attach the acetate to the stamped backing.

love coaster
set

Y̲ou know how love is sometimes found in the place where you least expect it? Well, inspiration for small tokens of love can be found in the strangest places, too. Recently, I tore some pages out of an old book to use as a base for one of my projects. As usual, I was examining the text to remove anything that might not be appropriate for the theme of the project. And then I thought, why not cut out the words to create my own sentences? Like a horse out of the gates, I was on a creative journey, exploring another great use for old books. I love it when these things happen! I formed expressions of love with my little cutout words, using old coasters as a base surface.

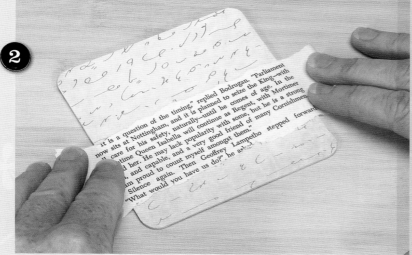

ONE. Cover coaster. Cover one coaster with a piece of decorative paper, using a glue stick to adhere the coaster in place. Remove any excess paper, using scissors to trim along the coaster edges.

TWO. Add next layer of paper. Tear a strip of coordinating decorative paper to fit across the coaster. (I tore a page from an old book.) Adhere the torn paper to the coaster with a glue stick, placing the strip where desired.

MATERIALS

square coasters

solid-colored cardstock

decorative paper
* black (7 Gypsies)
* script (Design Originals)

pages of an old book
(to be cut apart for text)

embellishments
* paper tag
* thin silk ribbon (Yarn Market)
* small rose embellishment
* game letter tiles (Limited Edition)
* additional embellishments of your choice, as desired

scissors

glue stick

tacky glue

sanding block

self-healing cutting mat

3

4

5

6

THREE. Add another layer of paper. Tear a narrower strip from another sheet of coordinating decorative paper. Using a glue stick, adhere this paper strip over the one already on the coaster.

FOUR. Create tag. Embellish a tag with decorative paper, using a glue stick to adhere the paper where desired. Trim any excess paper along the edges of the tag.

FIVE. Add tag to coaster. Using a glue stick, adhere the tag to the coaster, placing it on top of the layered paper strips. Tie a silk ribbon around a small decorative rose embellishment, then glue the rose on top of the tag with tacky glue. When finished, sand the edges of the coaster to distress them.

SIX. Cut out words. Decide what message you want to include in your design. Look through an old book and cut out words to spell out the message text. (You can also print the words on a computer using the font of your choice.) Cut out each word separately, then glue them onto a piece of colored cardstock. Trim around each word, leaving a slight border of color cardstock around it.

7

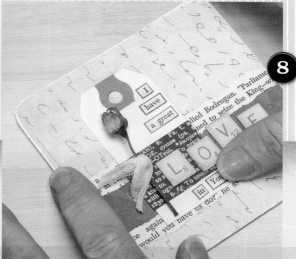

8

9

SEVEN. Add game letter tiles to coaster. Choose one word from your message that you want to emphasize. (I chose "love.") Select game letter tiles to spell out the word. Using tacky glue, glue the letters in place, layering them on top of the tag and the paper strips.

EIGHT. Add words to coaster. Glue the words from step 6 onto the coaster, positioning them above and below the game letter tiles.

NINE. Create matching coaster. Use your choice of coordinating paper and embellishments to create another coaster that is similar in style and theme to the first.

layers of possibilities

I thought it would be nice to express my love to my son in a totally different way. So I made this tag card for him, using his favorite outdoorsy colors. To create this card, cut the tag from chipboard, then cover it with paper. Cut words from book text and attach them to the tag. Finish it by adding stamps, tags, ribbon and baubles of your choice.

cherished memories
book

i have always been particularly proud of my husband's decision to serve our country in the marine corps. During his time in the service, I was happy to be his "dependant/wife," as I was called then. This period of our life together was the source of so many memories, from the beginning of our romance to the establishment of our family. We were apart for his two tours of duty, and with his absence came many letters that needed a home. After keeping and cherishing them for so many years, I made a book to preserve his letters, along with all the other memories from those days. This book represents the foundation of our love, which remains strong today.

layers

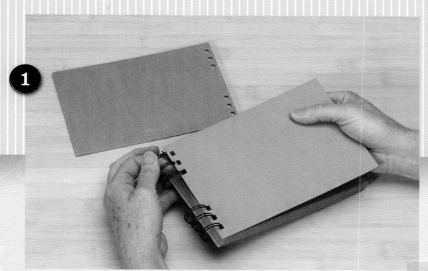

1

2

**spiral-bound journal
(7 Gypsies)**

decorative paper
* script (Autumn Leave)
* crème (Anna Griffin)
* green (Creative Imaginations)
* green script (Daisy D's)
* green stripe (American Traditional)
* crème embossed
  (Jennifer Collection)
* vellum (The Paper Company)

acetate

favorite photograph(s)

rubber stamps
* letters (Hero Arts)
* LOVE (My Sentiments Exactly)
* additional designs of your choice,
  as desired

ink
* solvent ink (Tsukineko StazOn Black)
* dye ink (Ranger Distress Inks)

embellishments
* word definition stickers
  (Making Memories)
* doorknob embellishment (7 Gypsies)
* rub-on letters (Autumn Leaves)
* paper tag
* decorative brads (Making Memories)
* ribbon
* skeleton key embellishment
  (K&Company)
* additional embellishments
  of your choice, as desired

paper trimmer

craft knife

scissors

Japanese screw punch

glue stick

double-sided tape

sanding block

pencil

hammer

self-healing cutting mat

ONE. Disassemble journal.
Disassemble a store-bought journal by opening the spiral binding and removing the covers and the pages.

TWO. Apply paper to covers.
Using a glue stick, adhere a sheet of decorative paper to the front cover. Trim any excess paper along the edges of the cover board. Then, cut a couple strips of coordinating decorative paper. (I embellished one strip by stamping it; see Tip, below.) Use a glue stick to adhere the paper strips to the left side of the front cover, then trim any excess paper along the edges of the board. Do not worry if you cover the binding holes along the left edge. Cover the back cover in the same manner.

TIP

You can create your own decorative paper by stamping it with words or text. Be sure to do the stamping before you glue the paper onto another surface. That way, you can trim the paper as needed without having to worry about running out of space. To match the romantic theme of the book, I stamped the word "LOVE" here.

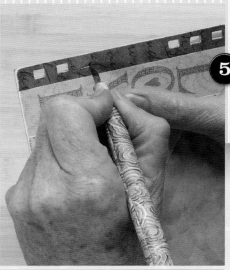

THREE. Create vellum pocket. Tear the upper right corner off a sheet of vellum. Place the torn sheet over the front cover, aligning the left edge of the sheet with the right edge of the decorative paper strip, as shown. Adhere the vellum along the bottom, left and right edges with double-sided tape, then trim any excess vellum along the edges of the cover. The top (torn) edge should remain untaped, creating a pocket.

FOUR. Cover tape. You can hide the double-sided tape that is visible through the vellum by adhering additional strips of decorative paper and text stickers along each edge of the cover.

FIVE. Poke holes. Distress the cover by running a sanding block along all four edges. Use a craft knife to neatly poke holes through the spiral binding holes on the left side of the front cover. ✱ **NOTE:** If you need to see where the holes are, hold the book cover up to the light. Light should pass through the existing holes, allowing you to see where to insert the craft knife.

SIX. Prepare cover for doorknob embellishment. Add any additional embellishments that complement the romantic theme, such as the "Cherish" sticker I placed along the top edge. Hold the doorknob embellishment up to the right edge of the book to determine proper placement. Mark the two points where the doorknob's brad prongs hit the surface of the cover, using a pencil. Use a screw punch to punch a hole through each mark.

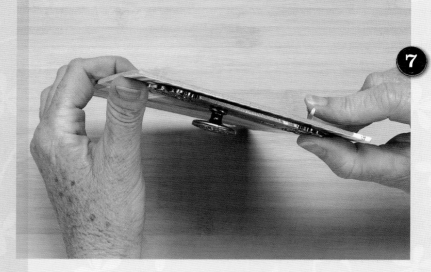

SEVEN. Secure doorknob. Insert the brads of the doorknob embellishment through the holes. Bend the brad prongs flush against the back of the cover, securing the doorknob panel in place. Use a hammer to tap the prongs against the surface of the cover.

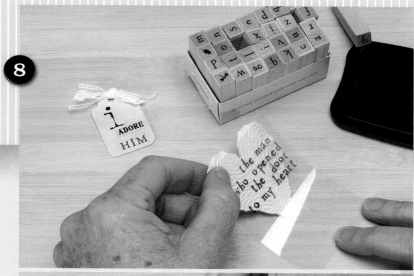

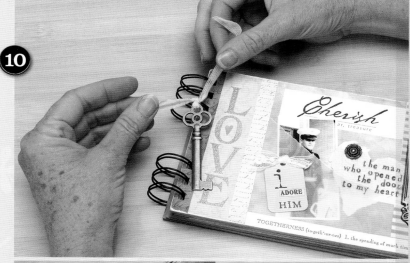

EIGHT. Create decorative elements. Using tags, stamps and stickers, make a few different text embellishments to match the design of the front cover. For one of the embellishments, tear a scrap of decorative paper into the shape of a heart. Stamp the text of your choice onto a piece of acetate with solvent ink, then attach the acetate to the heart with a decorative brad.

NINE. Add embellishments and reassemble book. Secure the embellishments to the front cover with ribbon, decorative brads or glue. Slip a favorite photograph or a meaningful note into the vellum pocket. Reassemble the book, inserting the front cover, interior pages and back cover through the spiral binding. Close the binding to secure.

TEN. Add key embellishment. With a length of ribbon, tie a skeleton key embellishment to the wire spiral binding.

ELEVEN. Cover and embellish interior pages. When finished with the front cover, select sheets of coordinating paper for the journal's interior pages. Cover each page with different colored and/or patterned paper, adding embellishments, stamps and photographs of your choice to match the theme and style of the cover.

childhood moments:

capturing memories
of growing up

When I was growing up, my grandparents liked to tell us stories about what the world was like for children of their era. The truth may have gotten stretched a bit here or there, but it was very intriguing all the same. I could have listened for hours. With this information, my sisters and I learned to appreciate what we experienced in our own lives and our own era.

Storytelling is folklore. As crafters, we have the ability to pass on stories through our art. These visual narratives give life to our memories, whether they are rooted in the long past of our grandparents' generation or the not-so-distant past of our children. In our own way, crafters participate in the folklore of today, creating layer upon layer of treasured stories.

Documenting childhood memories could seem like taming a wild horse. There is an overwhelming amount of details to consider, from the concrete components of color and pattern to the more conceptual themes of thoughts and emotion. This section makes the process fun, as it explores ordinary childhood moments as the basis for documenting and celebrating young lives. The projects vary, from weaving my own childhood memories into a special box for my mom to capturing moments of my son's life in a booklet. There are so many stories I never want to forget, and these projects capture those little gems in vivid detail.

babyface
frame

a child has so many expressions, which often make it difficult to capture his or her personality in just one shot. I had the opportunity to photograph my friends' daughter, Isabella, one afternoon. She was so cooperative and cheerful that day, allowing me to get some fun angled shots. When this photograph was developed, I loved it immediately and decided to make it into a gift for Isabella's parents. I found a simple, square, white-on-white frame, pretty just as it was but perfect with a bit of altering. With Isabella's character in mind, I began adding ribbon, paper and stamps until I arrived at a frame design befitting such an adorable face.

layers

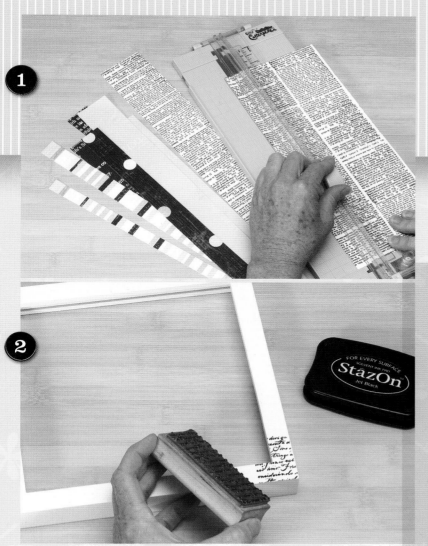

1

2

ONE. Cut paper strips. Cut strips of coordinating decorative paper to several different widths.

TWO. Stamp corner of frame. Remove the glass, mat and backing from the frame. Using solvent ink, stamp a design onto the lower right corner of the frame.

MATERIALS

frame, with glass, mat and backing board included

decorative paper
❋ pink patterns (Autumn Leaves)
❋ words in black (7 Gypsies)

favorite photograph

rubber stamp
❋ script (Hero Arts)

ink (Tsukineko StazOn Black)

ribbon, 3 types (Offray, May Arts)

paper trimmer

craft knife

scissors

tacky glue

double-sided tape

self-healing cutting mat

3

4

5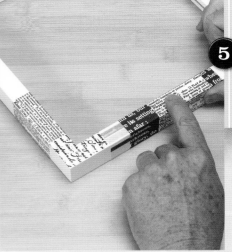

THREE. Glue paper to frame.
Flip one of the decorative paper strips over
so that it is face down on your work surface.
Along the top of the strip, apply tacky glue.
Position the glued-up end of the paper strip
inside the lip of the frame, then bring it
around to the front of the frame, burnishing it
in place with your hand.

FOUR. Secure paper to back
of frame. Once you have adhered and
burnished the paper strip to the front of the
frame, pull the remaining end of the strip
around to the back of the frame. Glue the strip
to the side and back of the frame, then trim
any excess paper with a craft knife.

FIVE. Add more paper strips.
Repeat steps 3–4 to add a few more strips of
decorative paper, covering the right rail of the
frame.

SIX. Add ribbon. For a little variety,
glue lengths of decorative ribbon around the
frame as you did the paper strips in step 5.

SEVEN. Create ribbon embellishment. Cut two lengths of the same ribbon, one about 3" (8cm) and the other about
2" (5cm). Tie the shorter ribbon around the
center of the longer length, finishing with a
simple knot.

6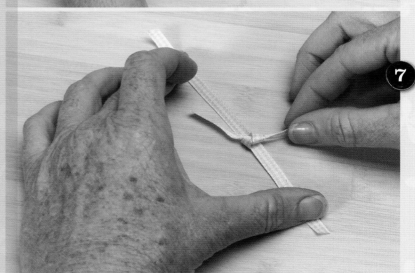

7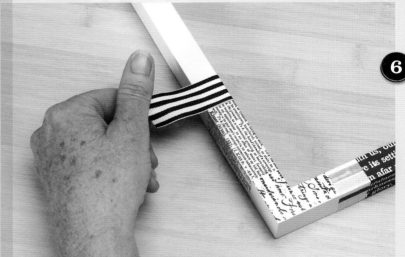

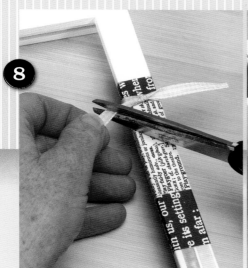

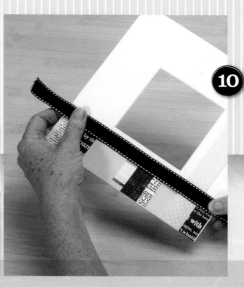

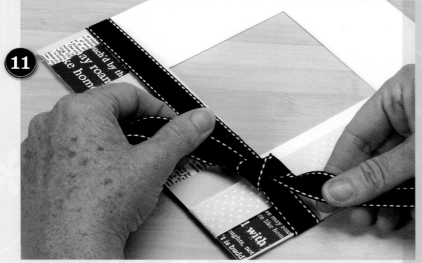

EIGHT. Attach ribbon to frame.
Position the knot around the right rail of the frame. When you are happy with the placement, attach the ribbon to the frame by adhering each end of the longer ribbon to the back of the frame with tacky glue. Trim each tail of the knot.

NINE. Add decorative paper to mat.
Place several coordinating decorative paper strips horizontally along the left side of the mat, and adhere them in place with double-sided tape. Use scissors to trim any excess paper along the left, top and bottom edges of the matboard.

TEN. Add lengths of ribbon to mat.
Run one length of decorative ribbon along the lower section of the mat, placing it parallel to the bottom edge. Wrap the ends of the ribbon around the edges of the matboard and adhere the ends to the back of the board with glue or double-sided tape. Then, add a length of another decorative ribbon along the left section of the mat, overlapping the first ribbon. Again, wrap the ends of the ribbon around the edges of the matboard, then adhere in place.

ELEVEN. Tie knot around ribbon. Cut a 4" (10cm) length of the same ribbon used along the left side of the mat. Tie it in a simple knot around the length of ribbon adhered to the matboard, as shown. Finish by trimming the ends.

TWELVE. Add photograph and assemble frame. Turn the mat over and, on the back surface, run a piece of double-sided tape along the top edge. Turn the mat back over and position the window over the photograph, cropping the image as desired. Press the mat onto the photograph to secure it in place. (Be aware that the photo will adhere to the tape.) Clean the glass. Insert the glass back into the frame, then insert the matted photograph. Close up the frame with the backing board.

unfolding
story tag

i came across these sweet photographs while rummaging through some old boxes that had belonged to my mother. Wanting to do something a little different than a scrapbook page, I considered what I especially liked about the two images— that they were taken within minutes of each other, documenting a tender moment between me and my father as it was unfolding. To capture that sentiment, I chose to highlight the pair in a little unfolding booklet, with some meaningful snippets of text attached. The base surface begins as a simple paper tag, but by the end of the project it is almost unrecognizable, having been transformed into a warm, inviting card.

1

2

ONE. Mark tag. Position a library pocket on a large paper tag, about 1" (3cm) from the end with the hole. (Once the library pocket is in place, there should be enough space left on the other side of the tag to fold it over and cover the pocket.) Run a pencil along each side of the library pocket to indicate its placement, then remove the pocket.

TWO. Cut paper for tag. Using the marked lines as a guide, fold in each side of the tag. The tag should now be divided into three panels. Trim two sheets of coordinating decorative paper—one sheet to fit over each end panel of the tag.

MATERIALS

large paper tag
(River City Rubber Works)

library pocket

decorative paper
* red/yellow stripes (Gazette)
* crème linen (Gazette, Daisy D's)
* script (7 Gypsies)
* burgundy stripes (7 Gypsies)

rubber stamps
* leaves (Hero Arts)
* words (Just Rite)

ink
* solvent ink (Tsukineko Staz-On Black)
* chalk ink (Clearsnap)

embellishments
* fabric words (MAMBI)
* button stickers (K&Company)
* small words (Design Originals Distressables)
* small metal clip
* small paper tag
* small envelope (Hero Arts)
* additional embellishments of your choice, as desired

two favorite photographs

ribbon (May Arts)

eyelets

paper trimmer

scissors

Japanese screw punch

eyelet setter and hammer

glue stick

double-sided tape

pencil

sewing machine

self-healing cutting mat

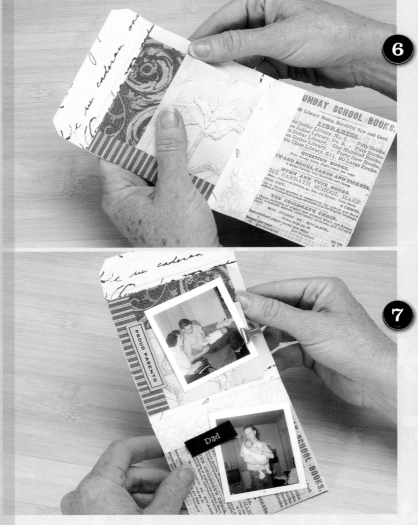

THREE. Stitch paper to panels.
Using a glue stick, adhere the paper to the tag's exterior end panels. Then, use a sewing machine to stitch the paper to the panel, running the stitch ⅛" (3mm) in from the edge of each panel.

FOUR. Cover tag interior. Cut several pieces of decorative paper to line the interior panels of the tag book. Use a glue stick to adhere the paper in place. Refold the tag, then trim any excess paper along the edges of the tag.

FIVE. Cover library pocket. Use a glue stick to cover the front panel of the library pocket with a few pieces of coordinating decorative paper. Trim any excess paper along the edges of the pocket.

SIX. Add pocket to panel. Using double-sided tape, adhere the library pocket to the interior center panel of the tag.

SEVEN. Embellish interior.
Decorate the interior of the tag with a photograph and your choice of stickers or other embellishments.

EIGHT. Add tag to interior. Stamp a paper tag with a favorite image or saying, then add it to the tag interior, securing it in place with double-sided tape.

NINE. Fill library pocket. Insert a photograph, tag or special message into the library pocket.

TEN. Embellish exterior. Close the tag by folding in the side panels. Decorate the exterior of the tag as desired, using tags, buttons, ribbons and other embellishments that coordinate with the interior. Punch a hole on the short flap, then set the hole with an eyelet. Wrap a ribbon around the folded tag, running one end of the ribbon through the eyelet. Tie the two ends of the ribbon together to secure the book shut.

layers of possibilities

I really enjoyed making this variation project—a tag booklet themed "A Child in the '60s." What fun I had going back in time and recalling fads and fashions from this era. Remember those aluminum Christmas trees? We had one, and I just had to include that as one of my memories! To make this project, form the tag into a matchbook-style, fold-out card. Inside, include a small pocket to hold tiny memento strips. Then adorn the book with ribbons and bows.

teenage
canvas

at fifteen, my son Scooter is in that stage that falls between "boy" and "man." I watch him as he goes through so many complicated changes, brought about by a sudden need to consider goals in self-image, academic success and life in general. As a tribute to his new growth in mind and body, I created a scrapbook page. With a strong masculine feel and soft boyish undertones, the design reflects Scooter's personality and his contrasting layers of "boy" and "man," which seem to emerge on a daily basis. His age serves as the subtitle, forever preserving this transitional time of his life. After completing the design, I turned the page into a piece of wall art by mounting it onto a canvas.

1

2

3

ONE. Apply paper to canvas.

Cut sheets of decorative paper into strips of various widths. Using a sponge brush, coat a portion of the canvas surface with découpage medium, then lay the paper strips across the canvas surface as desired. As you position the strips, leave about 2" (5cm) of paper to wrap around the edges of the canvas in the next step. Brush découpage medium over the paper strips, then burnish them to the surface with your finger.

TWO. Finish edges and corners.

Apply découpage medium to the surface of the canvas edges, making sure to apply plenty of medium to each canvas corner. Wrap the remaining 2" (5cm) of the paper strips around the edges. At each corner, make the strips meet so that the paper is glued together. Allow the medium to dry completely. Then, snip the excess paper flush along each corner, as shown.

THREE. Adhere excess paper to back.

Use tacky glue or découpage medium to adhere any excess paper to the back surface of the canvas frame, trimming and gluing to create mitered edges.

MATERIALS

12" × 12" (30cm × 30cm)
canvas (stretched and primed)

decorative paper
❋ script (7 Gypsies)
❋ crème embossed
   (Jennifer Collection)
❋ blues and greys (Basic Grey)

12" × 12" (30cm × 30cm)
**"Remember" transparency
(Daisy D's)**

favorite photograph

rubber stamps
❋ large letters
   (RiverCity Rubber Works)
❋ small letters (Hero Arts)

**ink (Tsukineko Staz-On
Brown)**

white acrylic paint

embellishments
❋ small wooden discs (EK Success)
❋ ribbon (Offray)
❋ brads (Making Memories)
❋ metal label holder (Magic Scraps)

paper trimmer

scissors

découpage medium

tacky glue

double-sided tape

adhesive dots

makeup sponge

craft sponge brush

self-healing cutting mat

FOUR. Add layers of paper to canvas. With découpage medium, adhere additional pieces of cut and torn paper onto the canvas, layering the paper as desired. Leave an ample space in the center to place the photograph.

FIVE. Add photograph. Position the photograph as desired over the layered paper, then adhere in place with double-sided tape.

SIX. Stamp words. Stamp the words of your choice around the photograph. (Here, I stamped "fifteen" using clear acrylic stamps inked with white acrylic paint that I applied with a cosmetic sponge.) Work backward, stamping the last letter first to avoid running out of space at the end of the word. From there, continue stamping the letters in reverse order, finishing with the first letter. Allow the paint to dry completely.

SEVEN. Place transparency over canvas. Place the "Remember" transparency over the canvas, lining up the edges of the transparency flush with the edges of the canvas. For embellishment, adhere two wooden discs to one corner of the transparency with adhesive dots (see Tip, below).

TIP

I stamped the wooden discs with "0" and "5" for the year the photo was taken.

layers

EIGHT. Prepare ribbon. Cut a length of ribbon long enough to fit around the canvas. Thread the ribbon through one side of a metal label holder, pulling about 1½" (4cm) of the ribbon through the frame opening. Poke a hole through both layers of the ribbon, then insert a brad and bend the two prongs back to secure. Do the same with another length of ribbon, again inserting and securing a brad.

NINE. Add ribbon. Adhere the ribbon to the transparency surface with adhesive dots. Run the ribbon around the edges of the canvas and secure to the back with tacky glue.

TEN. Adhere transparency to canvas. For security, adhere the upper left corner of the transparency to the upper left corner of the canvas with an adhesive dot.

ELEVEN. Stamp name. Personalize the design by stamping a name in the framed area with solvent ink. (I stamped "Scooter," which is my son's name.)

"how to raise a red head" book

as a toddler, Brooks, my red-headed son, started to show an avid but unusual interest in the natural world. This little boy liked to kiss the anchovies that we used for bait, wishing them a sweet "goodbye" as he flung them off the pier to their freedom. When we purchased a mackerel, also to be used for bait, he decided he had to keep it for himself (frozen) and play with it as a toy! I thought every mom raising a son shared the same challenges—until I learned that red heads seem to guarantee a unique adventure. I made this booklet for my son, now a teenager, who remains interested in nature and animals. To hold these rather unconventional child-hood memories, I chose an unconventional medium—a brown paper bag—to construct the book. The pages bring me back to those hysterical but tender times of raising a nature-loving fireball.

1

2

ONE. Stack and fold paper bags. Stack several brown paper lunch bags together (I used three), lining up the closed ends with the open ends in an alternating fashion. Fold the stack of bags in half, as shown here.

TWO. Punch holes along fold. Open up the folded bags, keeping them stacked. Use a pencil to make five evenly spaced marks along the inside fold. With an awl, punch a hole through each pencil mark.

MATERIALS

brown paper lunch bags

neutral, solid-colored cardstock (including cream)

decorative paper
* plaid (Chatterbox)

favorite photographs

embellishments
* coordinating ribbon and fibers (May Arts, Offray, Basic Grey)
* additional embellishments of your choice, as desired

rubber stamps

crochet thread

paper trimmer

scissors

awl

heavy needle

glue stick

double-sided tape (optional)

pencil

self-healing cutting mat

computer and printer

3

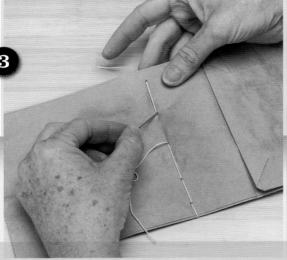

4

5

6

THREE. Run thread through spine. Thread a 15" (38cm) length of crochet thread onto a heavy needle. Starting from the exterior of the book, run the needle through the top hole, pinching the tail to prevent it from going through the hole. Pull the thread through to the interior, then run it through the next hole down, pulling it back out to the exterior. Continue running the thread into one hole and through the next until you reach the bottom hole. Then, run the thread in the same manner back up the spine to the top hole. When finished, knot the two tails of the thread together to secure the threaded spine.

FOUR. Adhere paper to cover. Cut a strip of decorative paper, making the width just a hair shorter than the width of the paper bag. Line up one end of the paper strip to the folded spine, and using a glue stick, adhere the paper to the front cover. Trim any excess paper along the right edge.

FIVE. Add more paper. Cut a sheet of cream cardstock, again making the width just a hair shorter than the width of the paper bag. Use a glue stick to adhere one end of the paper strip to the front cover, placing it about ½" (12mm) in from the right edge, as shown. Fold the remaining paper around the right edge and glue the paper to the interior surface of the front cover, trimming excess paper as necessary.

SIX. Print text. Using a computer and printer, generate and print a few words or sayings of your choice in different fonts on different colored cardstock. Use a paper trimmer to trim around the text.

layers

7

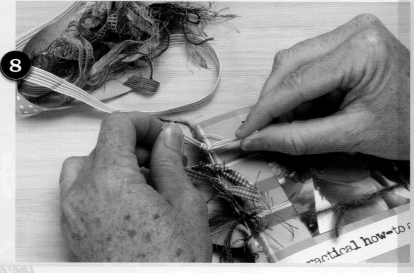

8

SEVEN. Decorate cover. Decorate the front cover, laying out your choice of text and images to create a pleasing composition. Use a glue stick and/or double-sided tape to adhere the text and images in place.

EIGHT. Tie ribbons to spine. Cut several 3" (8cm) lengths of coordinating decorative ribbon to match the front cover. Tie the ribbon lengths in a knot around each segment of crochet thread along the spine. When finished with the cover, decorate the interior pages with your choice of paper, text, embellishments, stamps and photographs.

the inside pages

Have fun completing the book, and feel free to make the interior pages as fancy as you want! I chose decorative paper and embellishments to match the style of the book's cover.

maternal memories
box

My mother is a very special lady. She is strong, gracious and kind, and she has endured so much in her lifetime. She is also a great source of inspiration. By nurturing my creativity, my mother has encouraged me to excel artistically. To show how much I cherish and love her, I have always wanted to make something unique for her—something that is as special as she is. So, I constructed this small box, which, when untied—surprise!—unfolds to reveal little drawers. Inside the drawers are handwritten messages, bearing thoughts and memories for my mother to read and treasure. I am a strong believer that we should express our feelings for loved ones before it is too late, and this project provides just the occasion to do so.

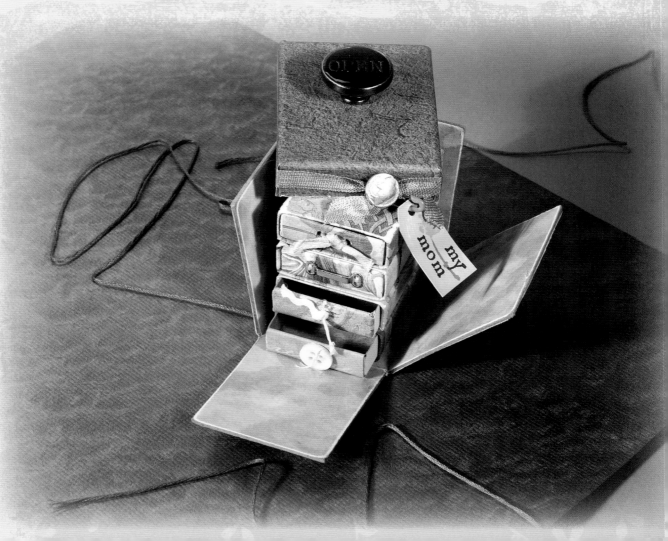

1

2

MATERIALS

collapsible box pattern, page 61

box lid pattern, page 61

chipboard

decorative paper
* soft green (Creative Imaginations)
* soft floral (K&Company)
* script (7 Gypsies)
* purple hyacinths (Paper Pizazz)
* green script (Daisy D's)

four matchboxes,
with slide-out interiors

rubber stamps
* small letters (Hero Arts)

ink (Tsukineko StazOn Black)

embellishments
* buttons
* ribbon
* decorative brad
* decorative safety pins
* small paper tag
* additional embellishments of
  your choice, as desired

book knob with
screw-in backing (7 Gypsies)

paper trimmer

craft knife

scissors

Japanese screw punch

glue stick

tacky glue

sanding block

screwdriver

self-healing cutting mat

photocopier

ONE. Cover box sides with paper. Transfer the collapsible box pattern onto chipboard, and cut apart the five pieces. (You can do this by photocopying the pattern, then tracing it onto chipboard.) Place a sheet of decorative paper face down on your work surface. Arrange the five chipboard pieces on the decorative paper, following the pattern arrangement. Where the pieces meet, butt the edges against each other. Adhere the chipboard pieces to the paper with a glue stick, then trim along the perimeter of the collapsible box chipboard unit, as shown. All of the chipboard pieces should remain on the same sheet, so do not separate the pieces by cutting the paper between the common edges.

TWO. Cover lid sides with paper. Transfer the lid pattern onto chipboard, and cut apart the five pieces. (Again, you can do this by photocopying the pattern, then tracing it onto chipboard.) Place a sheet of decorative paper face down on your work surface. Arrange the five chipboard pieces on the paper, following the pattern arrangement. Where the pieces meet, butt the edges against each other. Adhere the chipboard pieces to the paper with a glue stick, then trim along the perimeter of the lid chipboard unit. All of the chipboard pieces should remain on the same sheet, so do not separate the pieces by cutting the paper between the common edges.

THREE. Burnish chipboard units. When you are finished, flip the units over. Using the palm of your hand, burnish the decorative paper to the chipboard.

FOUR. Create covers for box and lid. Place another sheet of decorative paper face down on your work surface. Place the collapsible box chipboard unit on the paper and trace around the unit. Trim along the lines, but lengthen the end of each panel by about ¼" to ½" (6mm to 13mm), as shown. Do the same for the box lid unit, using a different kind of decorative paper.

FIVE. Place units on cover sheets. Place the covers created in step 4 face down on your work surface, then position each chipboard unit on its respective cover.

SIX. Begin covering lid. Use tacky glue to adhere the center panel of the chipboard lid unit to the center panel of its cover.

SEVEN. Finish covering lid. Apply glue stick to one flap of the lid cover. Bend the chipboard flap up, and while you are holding it upright, bring the cover flap up and adhere it the chipboard. Burnish the paper to the board. Adhere the cover flaps to the remaining chipboard flaps, each time adhering the paper while holding the flap upright.

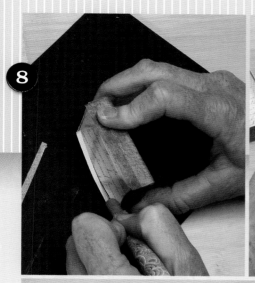

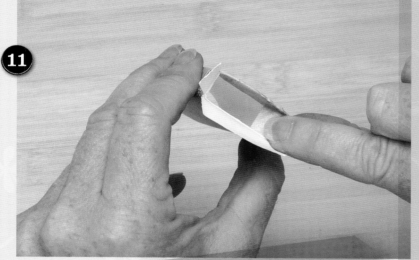

EIGHT. Trim excess paper. Use a craft knife to trim off any excess paper along the edge of each chipboard flap.

NINE. Cover collapsible box. Repeat steps 6–8 to cover the collapsible box chipboard unit. (For best results, see Creating Collapsible Movement, below.)

TEN. Cover matchbox. Remove the slide-out interior from a matchbox and put it aside for step 13. Cut a strip of decorative paper wide enough to cover the entire match-box, and 1" (3cm) longer than the length of the matchbox. With a glue stick, apply glue to the back of the paper strip. Center the matchbox on the paper, then wrap the paper around the exterior surface of the box, burnishing the paper around the edges.

ELEVEN. Tuck paper inside matchbox. Use a craft knife to slice the excess paper at the corners, making each cut follow the edge line. This will create four flaps on each end of the box. Run a glue stick over the inside surface of each flap, then tuck each flap into the box. Use your finger to burnish the paper to the inside surface.

creating collapsible movement

ONE. When applying glue to the paper flaps, also run your glue stick several times over each of the four folding edges, working the glue into the crevices.

TWO. When burnishing the paper to the board, use your thumbnail or fingernail to burnish the paper into the crease of each folding edge. These edges should remain foldable so that, after adhering the paper to the chipboard, you should still be able to move each side up and down.

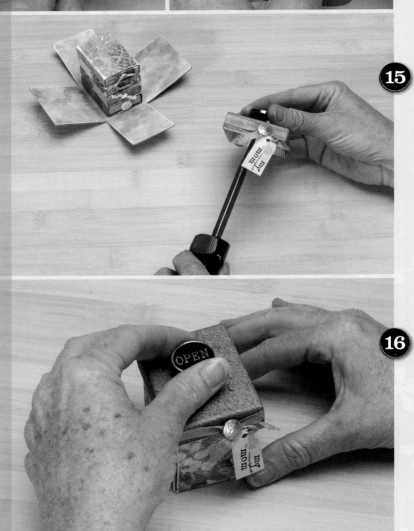

TWELVE. Complete stack of boxes.
Cover three more matchboxes, in the same manner.
Distress the edges of each box with a sanding block.
Stack the four matchboxes, gluing them one on top
of the other. Glue the stack to the center panel of the
collapsible box unit, positioning it so that its back is
flush to the back wall when upright, as shown.

THIRTEEN. Cover one box drawer. Cut
a strip of decorative paper to fit around the drawer of
one matchbox. Trim the strip to the width of the box,
then anchor it by gluing one end to the interior side
of one end. Wrap the paper around the bottom, gluing it to secure, and back to the interior of the oppo-
site end, as shown. Glue the paper to the interior,
and trim away any excess.

FOURTEEN. Finish drawers. Cover the
three remaining drawers in the same manner, using
different paper for each. When finished, slide one
drawer into each of the stacked matchboxes. Pull
the drawers in and out a few times to ensure smooth
movement. Using tacky glue, add fancy drawer pulls
made of buttons, ribbon or other embellishments.

FIFTEEN. Finish box lid. Add a few finishing
touches, such as ribbon, decorative brads, stamped
paper tags and other embellishments. Punch a hole
at the center point of the lid. Insert a book knob into
the hole, then twist the screw component onto the
knob from beneath the lid with a screwdriver.

SIXTEEN. Complete box. Insert handwritten
notes, images and other pieces of ephemera into
each of the box drawers. Slide the drawers shut.
Fold up the side panels of the box and secure the lid.
When you remove the lid, the sides of the box will
gently collapse to reveal the drawers within.

patterns

collapsible box pattern
Use a photocopier to copy this pattern at 100%.

box lid pattern
Use a photocopier to copy this pattern at 100%.

niece of mine

Generations

Grandmother

FAMILY 2 1

relationships that inspire:

treasuring family & friends

My life is much richer because of the people who surround and support me. Is it any wonder that friends and family serve as the main theme for most of my projects? They are the ones who have made me the person I am today. They help shape and inspire my creative spirit.

Friends weave into our lives like threads of joy. True friends are there when you need them, standing by you through thick and thin. But every friendship is different, because relationships vary from person to person. I find that each of my friends brings out something in me that mimics her own personality. I have very wacky friends who relate to my sense of humor. We have a great time no matter what we do, whether it's dying our hair together or sharing information about our aging bodies! When we get together, watch out—it's mayhem! Some of the best relationships I have are with my family, as they also fit into my circle of close friends. I am inspired by many members of my family, young and old alike.

This section is about treasuring those important relationships in your life, honoring those friends to whom you feel closest, and recognizing those people who have touched you, perhaps without even realizing it. I know that they are all a significant part of my being, having influenced me in one way or another. If you feel the same way, check out these projects, which give you the opportunity to express your feelings to those you adore most.

"niece of mine" memory page

i have a strong connection with my niece, who is not only a stunningly beautiful young woman but also my hero. At the age of twelve, she underwent surgery to correct her back, which had become malformed from scoliosis. During the surgery, the doctors fused fourteen of her vertebrae and inserted rods into her spine. My niece, throughout her recovery, proved to me and everyone around her that a positive attitude and sense of humor will get you through most anything in life. I have no doubt my niece's confidence, resiliency and personality will take her far! For her bold approach to life and her irrepressible charm, I honor my special girl with a bold and charming scrapbook page design.

niece of mine

1

2

ONE. Cut base paper and decorative paper. Using a paper trimmer, cut a base sheet of cardstock to 8" × 8" (20cm × 20cm), or your desired size for a memory page. Cut a few sheets of coordinating decorative paper into strips of varying widths.

TWO. Adhere decorative paper to base paper. Use a glue stick to adhere the decorative paper strips to the base cardstock, allowing the paper edges to meet or overlap as desired. ✽ NOTE: I used decorative gaffing tape to create one of the strips.

MATERIALS

solid-colored cardstock

decorative paper
✽ rusty script (7 Gypsies)
✽ gold stripes (Daisy D's)
✽ beige (Lasting Impressions)

decorative gaffing tape (7 Gypsies)

self-adhesive note paper

vellum

corrugated kraft paper

favorite photograph

rubber stamps
✽ letters (Hero Arts)
✽ flower (Hero Arts)

ink (Ranger Distress Ink)

embellishments
✽ round paper tag (Autumn Leaves)
✽ label staple (7 Gypsies)
✽ ribbon (May Arts)
✽ small metal hinge (Making Memories)
✽ decorative brads
✽ metal disc (Making Memories)
✽ flowers (Prima)
✽ small adhesive letters (Autumn Leaves)
✽ additional embellishments of your choice, as desired

paper trimmer

scissors

Japanese screw punch

glue stick

double-sided tape

adhesive dots

wooden skewer

mousepad

self-healing cutting mat

THREE. Stamp caption. Stamp a caption in the lower left area, leaving a space in the center for a photograph.

FOUR. Add photograph. Trim the photograph to size, then adhere it to the center of the page with adhesive dots or double-sided tape.

FIVE. Add embellishment. Add a decorative tag to the upper left corner of the page, and secure it in place with a giant label staple and ribbon.

SIX. Add hinge. Place a small hinge embellishment over the photograph and the page, lining up the center of the hinge with the right edge of the photograph. Holding the hinge in place, punch holes into the paper through each of the hinge holes. Run decorative brads through each hole, then flip the paper over and bend the brad prongs to secure the hinge in place.

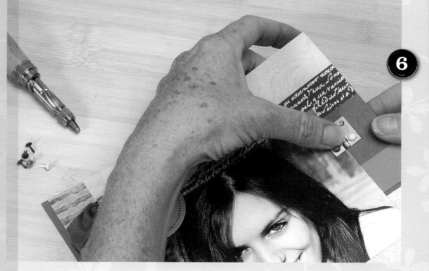

making an embossed tag

ONE. Stamp design.
Stamp an image onto a piece of self-adhesive note paper.

TWO. Emboss design.
Place the stamped note paper on a mousepad (or a swatch of fabric that has a little give to it). Cut a rectangular strip of vellum, then place the vellum over the stamped design. Use a wooden skewer to emboss the entire design, gently pressing the point of the skewer into the vellum. Take care not to puncture the paper when embossing; I first sanded down the point of the skewer so it wasn't too sharp.

THREE. Assemble tag. Cut a piece of corrugated kraft paper to the desired size and shape for a decorative tag. Then, adhere the embossed vellum to the tag, attaching it with adhesive dots. (Be sure the raised vellum surface faces out.) Because the dots will show through the vellum, try to place them in an area that will be covered by embellishments.

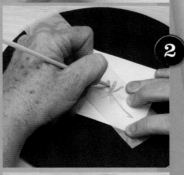

SEVEN. Make decorative tag.
Make an embossed vellum tag (see Making an Embossed Tag, at left). Decorate the tag with your choice of ribbons, metal discs, flowers and other embellishments.

EIGHT. Add final embellishments. Use adhesive dots or double-sided tape to adhere the embossed tag to the lower left corner of the page. Finish the page design with any final embellishments, such as letter stickers, along the upper right corner and anywhere else you desire.

clip-it
photo frame

it wasn't until I took this photograph that I truly recognized the maturity of my son Brooks. My intention was just to get a quick shot of him in his tux before going to the prom. Instead, I captured the real him—the boy that had somehow matured into a man, right under my nose. Because this was such a telling image, I felt that it warranted some kind of interesting treatment. So, I printed the photograph onto a transparency and set it over patterned paper. After mounting it to the clipboard, I noticed that, just under the lapel of Brooks' jacket—right where his heart is—there is an image of a young boy from the patterned paper beneath. What a perfectly appropriate layering of images, revealing the boy at heart within the man.

1

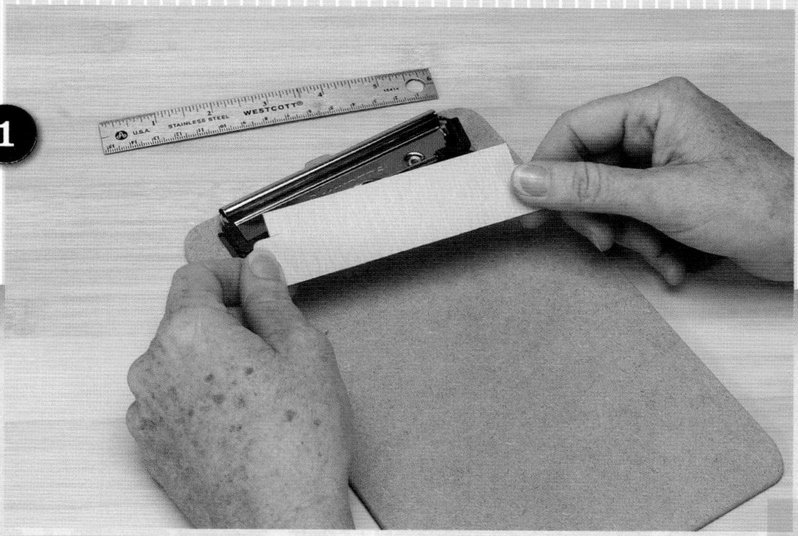

2

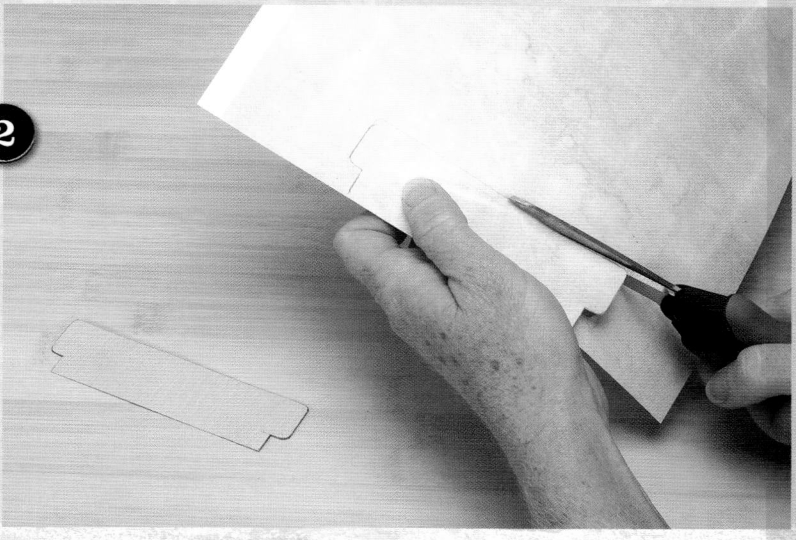

ONE. Draft template. Measure the dimensions of the metal clip portion on the clipboard and, using those dimentions, draft a corrensponding shape onto scrap paper. Cut out the shape with scissors. You are left with a tailored template for the paper you wish to mount to the clipboard.

TWO. Use template on decorative paper. Place a sheet of decorative paper face down on your work surface and center the top edge of the cutout shape along the top edge of the paper. Trace the shape, then cut it out. (Here, I used two-sided paper.) The paper will now fit perfectly around the metal portion of the clipboard.

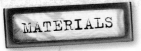

MATERIALS

- clipboard
- scrap paper
- decorative paper
  - ✻ (Design Originals)
- ink-jet transparency
- rubber stamps
  - ✻ flowers (Hero Arts)
- walnut ink (Walnut Liquid Stain)
- embellishments of your choice, as desired
- ribbon (May Arts)
- paper trimmer (I recommend a sliding trimmer)
- scissors
- glue stick
- double-sided tape
- adhesive dots
- sanding block
- ruler
- pencil
- self-healing cutting mat
- computer, printer and digital image

THREE. Apply paper to clipboard. Flip the decorative paper over so that it is pattern-side up. Tear off part of the bottom of the paper. Place the paper over the clipboard, fitting the cut area along the edges of the clip. Use a glue stick to adhere the paper to the board.

FOUR. Cover clipboard. Tear out pieces of coordinating decorative paper in varying shapes and sizes. Using a glue stick, adhere the torn pieces to the surface of the clipboard, layering and overlapping the edges. If desired, you can also stamp images onto some of the paper. (I stamped a couple of flower images with walnut ink.) When finished, distress the clipboard by sanding away some of the paper along the edges.

FIVE. Print and mount transparency. Print a favorite digital image on a transparency (see Tip, at right). Trim the transparency along the perimeter of the image. Choose a sheet of decorative paper on which to mount the image. Hold the transparency against the chosen paper to determine the proper placement of the image. The transparency is clear, so consider how the darker and lighter parts of the paper design will look against the darker and lighter parts of the image.

SIX. Attach transparency to paper. Use adhesive dots to tack the image to the decorative paper in the upper left and right corners. Try to place the dots in a dark area so that they are not visible through the transparency. After the two sheets have been secured to one another, trim the decorative paper flush with the edges of the transparency.

T I P

I printed the image from my computer, using transparency sheets made especially for an ink-jet printer. Alternatively, you could take an image to a local copy center and have them copy the image onto a transparency. If you print from your own computer, use the formatting tools of your software to create a mirror image. This will allow the image and any accompanying text to be printed in reverse. The transparency can then be mounted right-side down, protecting the ink from smears or scratches and allowing the viewer to read the text correctly. It is not necessary to flip the image if you are taking it to a copy center because copier ink is permanent.

7

8

9

SEVEN. Add paper strip to transparency. Cut a strip from a sheet of decorative paper to fit over the top edge of the transparency. Adhere the strip to the transparency with double-sided tape.

EIGHT. Clip image to board. Attach the transparency to the board, placing the paper strip under the clip to secure it in place. Tie a length of decorative ribbon around the board just below the clip, and finish with a bow.

NINE. Add final embellishments. Adhere your choice of embellishments to the frame for a final touch. I kept it simple and used a glue stick to adhere just a strip of decorative paper below the image.

layers of possibilities

Sons are not the only ones who surprise you with their transformation from boy to man. The firefighter pictured in this variation project is a young man who is near and dear to my heart. I have known him since he was ten years old, and I have enjoyed watching him change over the years. To honor his courageous career choice of firefighter/ paramedic, I made a clipboard frame and titled it "No Fear."

clearly friendship
card

good friends are an integral part of our lives. They are there to listen, encourage and lend advice when we need it. And, sometimes, they don't even need to do *anything*—they can make our lives richer simply by being themselves. I have been extremely blessed to find best friends in my sisters. We know each other through and through, we understand each others' feelings, and we communicate clearly without fear of judgment. For this reason, I felt it would be appropriate to use a transparent acetate base for a friendship card, representing the open, respectful and "perfectly clear" nature of our relationship.

1

2

ONE. **Cover slide mount.** Cover both sides of a slide mount paper frame with decorative paper. To do so, run a glue stick over the front surface of the frame, then lay the paper down over the surface and burnish. Using a craft knife, trim any excess paper along the edges of the frame and trim out the interior window. Repeat the process, covering the back surface in the same manner.

TWO. **Stamp frame.** Stamp the paper-covered frame with the word of your choice.

MATERIALS

decorative paper
* numbers and letters (Creative Imaginations)

acetate or transparency

slide mount paper frame (Design Originals)

cardstock notecard (optional)

rubber stamps
* fancy script (Hero Arts)
* letters (My Sentiments Exactly)

ink (Tsukineko StazOn Black)

embellishments
* ribbon (EK Success, Adornments)
* decorative tag (I kan'dee)
* flowers (Prima)
* rivet stickers (EK Success)
* additional embellishments of your choice, as desired

paper trimmer (I recommend a sliding trimmer with a scoring attachment)

craft knife

scissors

Japanese screw punch

glue stick

adhesive dots or double-sided tape

scoring tool (if not attached to paper trimmer)

burnishing tool (such as bone folder, craft knife handle or pencil)

soft tissue or cloth

self-healing cutting mat

3

4

friends

5

THREE. Stamp acetate. Using solvent ink, stamp a fancy script design about 1" (3mm) from the right edge and bottom edge of a sheet of acetate (see Tip, at right).

FOUR. Score acetate. The stamped design will appear on the front of the card. Keeping this in mind, determine where you need to score the acetate to make it a folded card. Score accordingly with a scoring tool. (In this image, I am using the scoring attachment of a paper trimmer.)

FIVE. Fold card. When finished scoring, fold the acetate sheet along the score line. Run a burnishing tool along the fold to create a crisp crease.

SIX. Trim card. Once the card is folded, you may need to trim the interior panel of the card. If so, trim the right side of the card as needed.

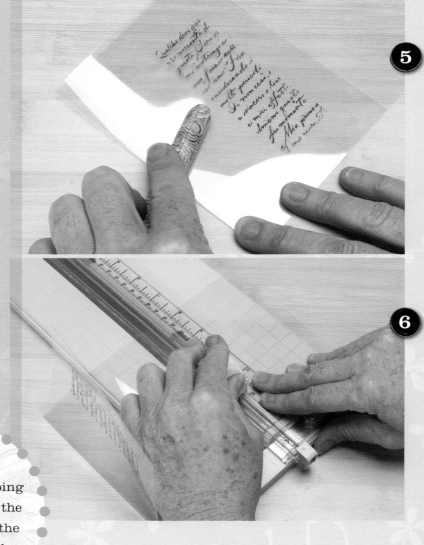

6

T I P

Be very steady when you are stamping on acetate. Because the surface is so slick, the stamp can slip easily.

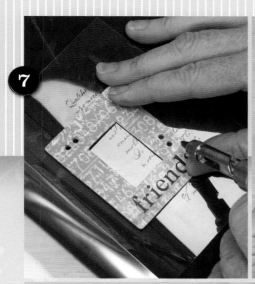

SEVEN. Punch holes. Position the slide mount frame on the front of the acetate card as desired. Once it is in position, use a screw punch to punch four holes (two sets of two holes each) through the frame and the acetate, as shown.

EIGHT. Attach slide mount to acetate. Run a length of ribbon through one set of holes on the acetate, adjusting it so that the two tails of the ribbon are equal. Run the ribbon through the corresponding holes on the slide mount.

NINE. Secure slide mount to acetate. Slide a small decorative tag or other embellishment onto the ribbon, then tie the ribbon in a knot, securing the slide mount and tag to the acetate. Run another ribbon through the second set of holes, fastening the slide mount to the acetate in the same manner.

TEN. Add embellishments. Place flowers or other small embellishments inside the slide mount window, adhering them to the acetate with adhesive dots or double-sided tape.

ELEVEN. Wipe acetate clean. Use a soft tissue or cloth to wipe smudges and fingerprints off the acetate. If desired, write a personalized note on a notecard, then slip it inside the acetate card.

electrical outlet
plate frame

Sometimes you find the best ideas in the most unexpected places. I had a box of unused electrical outlet plates in my basement, and I was just about to get rid of them when I came up with a great idea—I could use the plates as picture frames! The result was this charming accordion-style frame. I have inserted images of my son and my niece, who have become such good friends over the years that they are like brother and sister. I couldn't have chosen a more appropriate frame for this outgoing dynamic duo, because when they get together, they create quite a power surge!

①

②

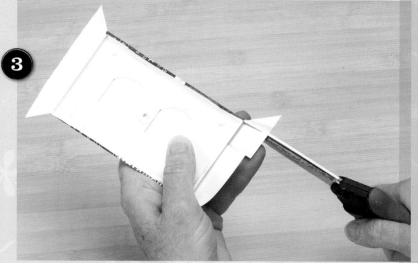

③

five electrical outlet plates

solid-colored cardstock (pink)

decorative paper
* black and whites (7 Gypsies)
* pinks (Autumn Leaves)

small photographs

coordinating ribbon (May Arts, Offray)

rubber stamps
* script (Hero Arts)
* additional designs of your choice

ink (Tsukineko StazOn Black)

embellishments
* metal scrapbook tags (7 Gypsies)
* epoxy stickers (Autumn Leaves)
* charms (I kan'dee)
* decorative brads (Making Memories)
* additional embellishments of your choice

paper trimmer

craft knife

scissors

glue stick

tacky glue

self-healing cutting mat

ONE. **Cover plate and cut paper.** Cut several square and rectangular pieces of decorative paper. Using tacky glue, cover the front surface of an electrical outlet plate with the decorative paper, layering pieces and overlapping edges. Allow the excess paper to extend beyond the edges of the plate. When the plate is completely covered, turn the plate over and place it face down on your work surface. Using a craft knife, slice a diagonal line through the excess paper to each corner point, as shown.

TWO. **Fold paper around the edges.** On the right and left sides of the plate, glue and burnish the paper to the sloping edges. Then, fold the excess paper around to the back surface.

THREE. **Trim excess paper.** With the outlet plate face down, use a craft knife to trim away the excess paper about ⅛" (3mm) from the left and right edges. Then, using scissors, trim the remaining excess paper on the top and bottom so that the paper edges align with the plate edges, as shown.

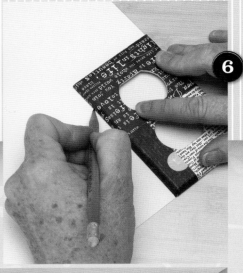

FOUR. **Finish edges.** Along the top and bottom of the plate, glue and burnish the paper to the sloping edges. Then, fold the excess paper around to the back surface. With the outlet plate face down, use a craft knife to trim away the excess paper about ⅛" (3mm) from the left and right edges.

FIVE. **Cut out windows.** Using a craft knife, cut along the edges of the socket holes to create windows in the plate.
✱ **NOTE:** If you need to see where the edges of the socket holes are, hold the plate up to the light. Light should pass through the existing holes, allowing you to see where to insert the craft knife.

SIX. **Create plate backing.** Place the plate on a piece of cardstock, then trace around the perimeter, as shown. Cut the rectangular shape out of the cardstock, trimming along the lines.

SEVEN. **Make embellishments.** Create or prepare embellishments small enough to be displayed inside the windows. For this particular plate, I stamped a script design onto a piece of cardstock, then inserted it into a metal scrapbook tab.

EIGHT. **Adhere embellishments to backing.** Lay the embellishments and photos of your choice on the cardstock backing. Hold the plate over the cardstock and adjust the placement of the embellishments to align with the socket holes. Glue the embellishments in place to the cardstock.

⑨

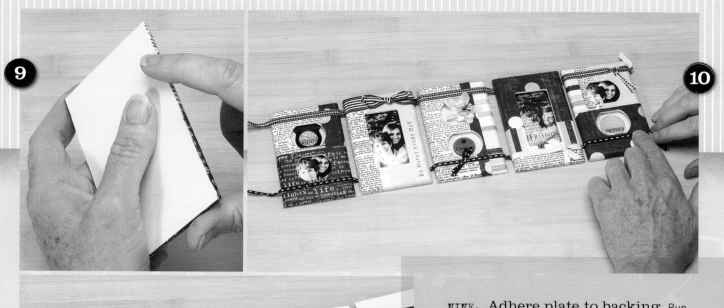

⑩

⑪

⑫

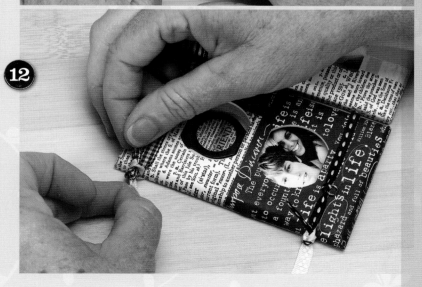

NINE. Adhere plate to backing. Run tacky glue along the back edges of the plate, then press the plate onto the cardstock so that the windows frame the embellishments. If necessary, use a craft knife to trim the cardstock along the edges. Turn the plate over and run your finger along each edge to burnish the backing in place.

TEN. Make four more plates and connect. Use coordinating paper, stamps, stickers, charms, decorative brads and other embellishments of your choice to create four more plates, repeating steps 1–9. Place all five plates side by side in a horizontal row, leaving about ½" (13mm) between each. Cut a 20" (51cm) length of ribbon, then attach the plates to each other by weaving and gluing the ribbon along the front of one plate and then behind another, positioning the ribbon about ½" (13mm) from the top edges. Cut another 20" (51cm) length of ribbon, and do the same, this time positioning the ribbon about ½" (13mm) from the bottom edges. Allow about 2" (5cm) of each ribbon to hang off the left edge of the first plate. Let the glue dry completely. After the plates are secure, you can add more ribbon embellishments.

ELEVEN. Add ribbons to first plate. Turn the hinged plates face down on your work surface. Cut two lengths of ribbon and glue them to the back of the first plate, aligning them with the ribbon end hanging off the front of the plate.
✱ NOTE: When the plates are face down, with the bottom edge facing you, the "first plate" will be the plate on the far right.

TWELVE. Finish with bows. Turn the hinged plates back over so they are face up on your work surface. Tie each set of ribbon ends in a bow along the left edge of the first plate. The hinged plates can be displayed standing accordion-style.

"my three men" book

the three men in my life are my husband, Tom, and my sons, Brooks and Scooter. This project is all about my "three men"—my true loves, my life, my everything. It has been such an amazing experience to witness their changes over the years and the friendship they have developed with each other. I want this stage in life to last forever! But realistically, I need to just celebrate a job well done as I begin to let go and release my sons into the world. In this book, I have tried to capture each of my men individually at this moment in time so that, later in life, I'll be able to reflect upon these happy days.

1

2

ONE. Cut cardstock. Open one of the compact disc pocket folders and measure the cover panel from the left edge to the right edge. Cut a sheet of cardstock just a hair smaller than the overall dimensions of the cover panel.

TWO. Score cardstock. With the pocket folder still open, measure from one edge of the cover to the first fold at the center. Measure and mark a line at the same distance from the edge of the cardstock. Score the paper along the line.

MATERIALS

two blank compact disc pocket folders (River City Rubber Works)

solid-colored cardstock

decorative paper
　✷ blues/bold patterns (Basic Grey)
　✷ script (Autumn Leaves)

page from an old book (to be torn apart)

denim

ribbon or fabric trim

favorite photographs

rubber stamps
　✷ flowers (Hero Arts)
　✷ heart (Hero Arts)
　✷ scroll (handmade)
　✷ additional designs of your choice, as desired

ink (Ranger Distress Ink)

white acrylic paint

embellishments
　✷ folder tab
　✷ paper tag

　✷ miniature decorative frames (Scrap Works)
　✷ rub-on letters (Autumn Leaves)
　✷ letter stencils
　✷ lettered metal charms
　✷ buttons
　✷ additional embellishments of your choice, as desired

paper trimmer

scissors

glue stick

tacky glue

double-sided tape

scoring tool

plastic card for burnishing (such as a credit card or hotel key card)

sanding block

makeup sponge

label maker (Dymo)

ruler

self-healing cutting mat

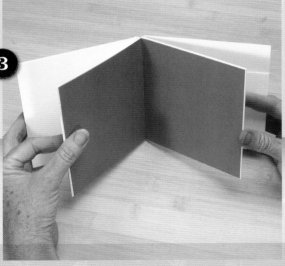

3

4

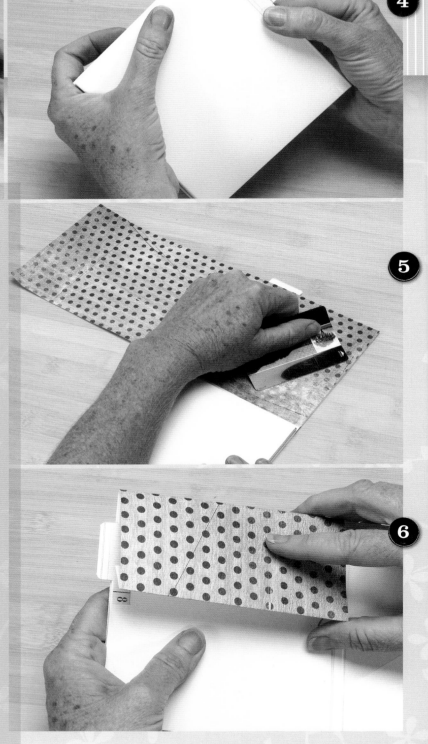

5

6

THREE. Hinge cases together.
Close the two pocket folders, then lay them
face down on your work surface, spine to
spine. Use double-sided tape to adhere the
cardstock across both back covers, forming a
hinge. This will join the two folders to create
one unit.

FOUR. Add tab to cover. Use a glue
stick to adhere a folder tab to the inside surface of the front cover panel, along the upper
right side.

**FIVE. Line front and back cov-
ers with paper.** Cover the front of the
folder booklet with decorative paper, using a
glue stick or double-sided tape. When applying the paper, place it so that at least 3½"
(9cm) of excess paper hangs off the top edge,
as shown. Burnish the paper to the cover with
the edge of a plastic card, such as a credit
card, as shown. Cover the back of the booklet
with coordinating decorative paper. Burnish
with a plastic card, then trim any excess paper
along the edges of the back panel.

SIX. Create interior flap. Wrap the
excess decorative paper over the top edge of
the front cover, forming a flap on the cover's
interior. Trim the flap so that it measures 3½"
(9cm). For a finished look and sturdier edge
line, fold an additional 1" (3cm) of paper under
and behind the flap.

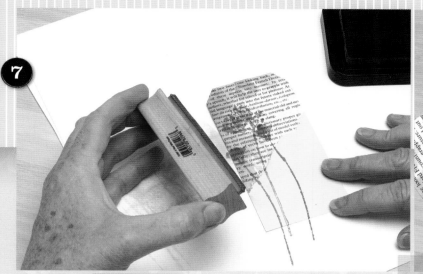

SEVEN. Create decorative tag.
Tear a page from an old book, then use a glue stick to adhere the torn piece to one area of a paper tag. Trim off any excess paper along the tag's edges. Give the torn page an aged look by staining the edges with ink. Stamp an image onto the tag, allowing the image to print over the book page and off the edges of the tag.

EIGHT. Trim tag. Using a glue stick, adhere a strip of decorative paper about ³⁄₄" (19mm) from the bottom of the tag. Trim the tag, cutting the bottom flush with the edge of the decorative paper strip.

NINE. Apply paint to tag. Use a sanding block to roughen up the surface of the decorative paper strip. Load a makeup sponge with white acrylic paint, then apply a light, uneven layer of paint to the paper strip.

TEN. Embellish tag. Add your choice of embellishments to the tag. If you'd like to add text to the tag, create words with rub-on letters, stamps, stencils or lettered charms.

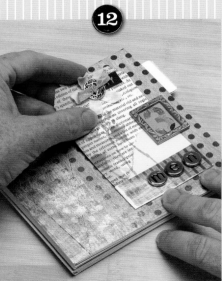

ELEVEN. Finish tag. Finish the tag with additional embellishments, such as buttons, ribbons and handmade labels (see Tip, below).

TWELVE. Secure tag to cover. Adhere the decorative tag to the front cover with double-sided tape, placing the tag about ½" (13mm) from the right edge.

THIRTEEN. Ink stamp. Choose a decorative stamp that is about as long as the spine of the booklet. (I made my own stamp for this step; see page 14 for more information.) Load a makeup sponge with white acrylic paint, then tap the sponge onto the rubber surface until the stamp is fully "inked" with paint.

FOURTEEN. Stamp design onto denim. Press the inked stamp onto a piece of denim, cut to fit along the spine of the booklet. Allow the paint to dry completely.

T I P

One of my favorite embellishment techniques is creating title labels with my label maker. This handy little device is so easy to use, and it promises great results every time. I love that the letters are white on a colored background.

layers

15

16

FIFTEEN. Glue denim to spine.
Use tacky glue to adhere the stamped denim onto the spine of the book, centering the design along the spine, as shown.

SIXTEEN. Finish cover. Open the book and trim the top and bottom ends of the denim flush with the edges of the book. Using tacky glue, add a decorative ribbon or trim parallel to the spine, covering the rough edge of the cut denim. Once the cover is complete, fill the interior pages with your choice of stamps, photographs and embellishments.

the inside pages

In this booklet, each of my three men got his own page. When I am making a book, I always try to maintain a similar style while giving every page its own personality.

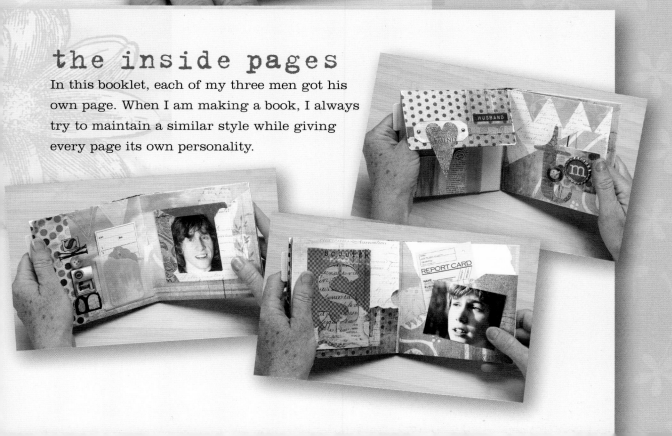

days gone by:

documenting the past

the past provides endless inspiration for my projects. After all, history is made up of countless layers, all of them colorful and compelling. When we peel these layers away, we realize just how much we have to learn from history, whether it is that of our own family, our nation or our planet. Those who went before us, family members and historical figures alike, have great experiences to share with us—and great experiences can be transformed into great project ideas. So, I have decided to dedicate this section to the past.

I feel a natural attraction to objects with an aged appearance. Some things, like the antiques that furnish my home, *are* actually old, while others, like the photographs I take or the papers I work with, just *look* old. Either way, the beauty of "the old" calls out to me, begging me to hear its story. Behind a spot of rust or a little dust, I know there is a hidden treasure. It may be primitive but surprisingly practical; it may be obsolete but wonderfully unique; it may be faded but rich in possibilities.

From scrapbook pages to miniature tribute books, every project in this section features some aspect of years gone by. In one way or another, we all lay claim to a different bit of history. So, use your own stories and memories for personal inspiration, and feel free to explore the vintage materials that I find so exciting—outdated office supplies, antique images or aged photos evoking a fond or funny memory.

vintage image
bracelet

i have always been attracted to vintage style and ephemera, and it shows in every aspect of my life—my art, my home décor, my fashion. Yes, I love it enough to wear it, and this creative bracelet offers the perfect opportunity to do so! I had been holding onto a sheet of small, classic photographs of women for some time. While browsing through a craft store one day, I came upon this bracelet, and I knew exactly how I wanted to use it: to create a unique accessory with vintage flair. With a quick addition of ribbon, beads or dangles, it was easy to give this bracelet a custom touch.

layers

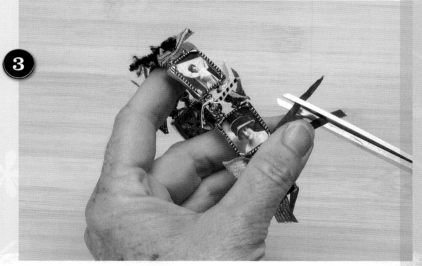

ONE. Cut out vintage images.
Remove the acetate pieces from each bracelet square. Cut out the vintage images, trimming each to fit inside one bracelet square.

✱ **NOTE:** Because the acetate pieces are transparent, they can serve as handy guides for cropping and trimming the images.

TWO. Insert images. Insert the trimmed images into the bracelet squares, then secure the corresponding pieces of acetate on top.

THREE. Embellish with ribbons.
Cut several lengths of coordinating ribbon and fibers. Tie the ribbon around each set of links on the bracelet. When finished, trim the ends of the ribbon as desired.

MATERIALS

bracelet with square frame links (each frame fitted with a piece of removable acetate)

small vintage photographs (ArtChix Studios)

fibers and ribbons (May Arts, Offray, Yarn Market)

scissors

self-healing cutting mat

library pocket
card

to combine two of my favorite elements—a collage technique and a vintage style—is bliss! In this project, these two elements work together to generate a warm, even humorous design. From funny antique images to old book pages, the materials I use for this card reflect my love for the past. I find great inspiration at a little store near my house that sells unique and often outdated office supplies, such as library pockets (used here), sales tags, adding machine tape and rolls of tickets. I suppose I find as much comfort as I do inspiration in using these unusual materials from days gone by.

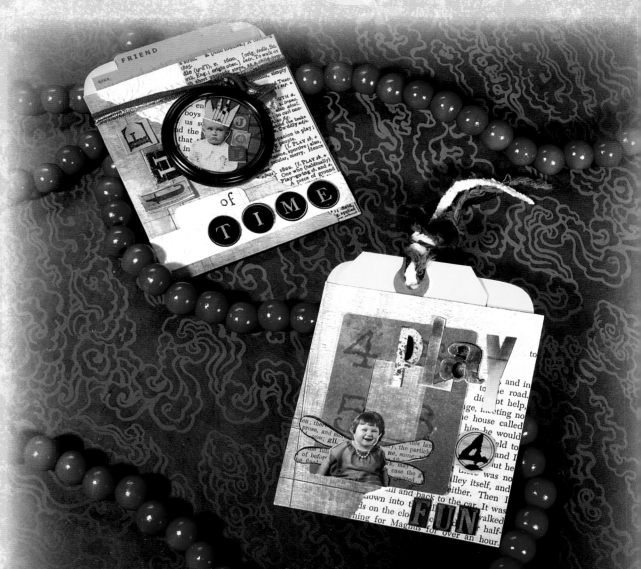

layers

1

2

ONE. Cover pocket panel. Tear a few pieces of decorative paper. Use a glue stick to adhere the torn paper to the front panel of a library pocket, layering and over-lapping the edges. Trim the excess paper along the edges of the pocket.

TWO. Cover small frame. Using a glue stick, adhere a piece of decorative paper to the front of a slide mount frame. With a craft knife, trim any excess paper along the edges of the frame, then trim out the window.

MATERIALS

library pockets

decorative paper
* orange mix (Basic Grey)
* blue (Basic Grey)
* brown (7 Gypsies)
* crème embossed
  (Jennifer Collection)

**slide mount paper frame
(Design Originals)**

**pages from an old book
(to be torn apart)**

**definition card
(Autumn Leaves)**

rubber stamp
* letters (Hero Arts)
* #4 (My Sentiments Exactly)
* additional designs of your choice,
  as desired

ink (Ranger Distress Ink)

embellishments
* paper letters (Daisy D's)
* vintage children images
  (Design Originals)
* paper tags
* ribbons
* letter stickers (EK Success)
* miniature round frame (I kan'dee)
* additional embellishments of
  your choice, as desired

craft knife

scissors

glue stick

double-sided tape (optional)

self-healing cutting mat

3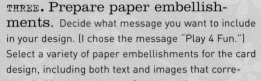

 **4**

THREE. Prepare paper embellish-ments. Decide what message you want to include in your design. (I chose the message "Play 4 Fun.") Select a variety of paper embellishments for the card design, including both text and images that correspond with your message. Cut out each embellishment.

FOUR. Add first layer. Use a glue stick or double-sided tape to adhere the paper-covered frame to the front panel of the pocket. Then, adhere the first layer of paper embellishments (here, the letters) to the panel where desired.

FIVE. Add next layer. Adhere the second layer of paper embellishments (here, the images) to the panel where desired.

SIX. Stamp panel. Once you have finished applying the paper embellishments to the card, stamp a decorative element onto the panel. (I stamped the number 4 to complete the message "Play 4 Fun.")

 **5**

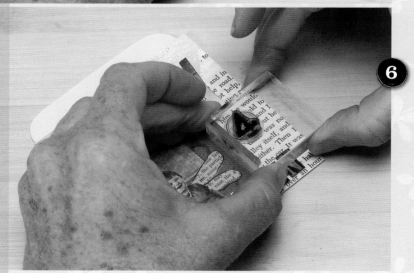 **6**

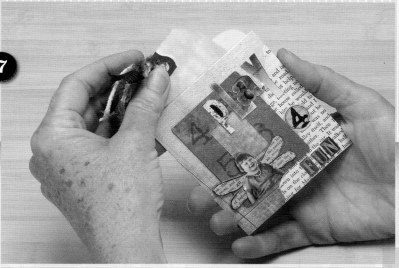

7

8

9

SEVEN. Insert tag. Create a personal-ized tag or card, embellishing to coordinate with the design of the library pocket. Tie a ribbon on one end of the tag to serve as a pull, then insert the tag into the pocket.

EIGHT. Create another card. Use coordinating decorative paper to make anoth-er pocket card as a mate for the first. (For this card, I chose to incorporate the message "The Joy of Time.") Decorate the card with your choice of stamps, stickers, tags, images, frames and other embellishments.

NINE. Insert card into pocket. Complete the second card by inserting a defi-nition card (or handmade tag) into the pocket.

layers
of possibilities

The look of this clear pocket was just scream-ing for something very nostalgic. So, I stamped and colored an image of a soldier, cut it out, then mounted it to a great background paper. I stamped the man's face onto a piece of acetate and painted his eyes and mustache from the back with acrylic paints. Feel free to choose your own image and embellishments for a variation project like this.

little book of
inspiration

Most of my "years-gone-by" projects document stories, memories and people from my own life. But, every once in a while, I like to honor more general figures from the past, those people who touched my life even though I never knew them. One example are the suffragists, those strong, persevering ladies who pioneered a path for all womankind so many years ago. I have made a mini book to commemorate the efforts of the gutsy women who walked before me, fighting tenaciously for the rights and the privileges we enjoy (and often take for granted) today. I'd like to salute their huge role in history by incorporating their spirit into this little altered book of inspiration.

layers

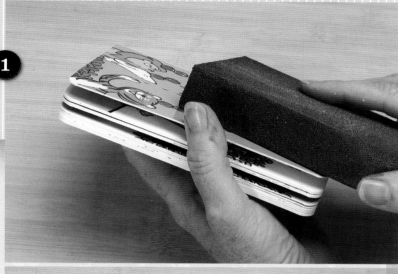

1

2

ONE. Sand book pages. Use a sanding block to roughen the surface of each page of the board book, sanding away the finish if it is glossy.

TWO. Cover front and back covers. Using a glue stick, adhere a piece of decorative paper to the front cover of the book. Trim the paper along the edges and rounded corners of the cover, as shown. Cover the back of the book, and trim in the same manner.

MATERIALS

board book with thick pages (such as a children's book)

decorative paper
❋ crème brown (Daisy D's)
❋ brown numbers
❋ newspaper (7 Gypsies)
❋ script (Karen Foster)

large paper tag

acetate or transparency

rubber stamps
❋ numbers and letters (Hero Arts)
❋ "No Regrets" (River City Rubber Works)
❋ additional designs of your choice, as desired

ink (Tsukineko StazOn Black)

white acrylic paint

cosmetic sponge

embellishments
❋ snap (Dritz)
❋ wire-looped photo holder (7 Gypsies)
❋ ribbon
❋ metal scrapbooking tab (7 Gypsies)
❋ old suffragist-related images
❋ ephemera (MAMBI)

paper trimmer

scissors

glue stick

tacky glue

double-sided tape

sanding block

stapler

self-healing cutting mat

3

4

5

6

7

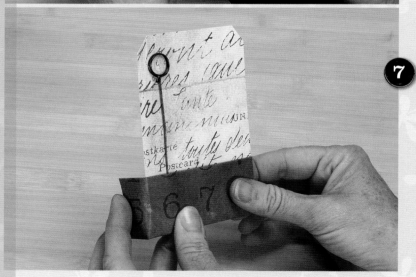

THREE. **Cover spine.** Cut a strip of decorative paper that coordinates with the cover. Trim the strip to the same length as the book. Apply glue with a glue stick to the back of the paper strip, then center it over the spine, as shown. Use your fingers to burnish the paper onto the cover and around the edges.

FOUR. **Add snap clasp.** With tacky glue, adhere one snap embellishment onto the front of the cover, placing it at the center of the right edge, as shown. Glue the matching snap embellishment in the same place on the back cover to form a snap clasp.

FIVE. **Prepare paper tag.** Create a flap by folding up the bottom 1½" (4cm) of a large paper tag.

SIX. **Embellish tag interior.** Use a glue stick to adhere decorative paper to the area on the tag above the fold. Trim the paper along the edges of the tag. Hold the tail of a wire-looped photo holder to the tag, as shown, and staple in place. If the wire tail extends beyond the fold, bend it into an L shape so that you can fold up the bottom flap.

SEVEN. **Finish pocket.** Cut a strip of decorative paper that is about 1" (3cm) wider than the bottom flap and about 2" (5cm) longer. Place this strip on the flap so that it extends about 1" (3cm) beyond each side edge and about 1" (3cm) beyond the bottom edge. Fold the paper over the bottom edge and glue the paper to the back of the tag. Then, fold the paper over each side edge and glue the paper to the back of the tag. You should now have a pocketed tag.

8

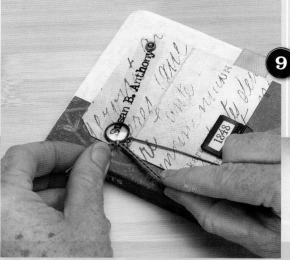

9

EIGHT. Stamp cover. With double-sided tape, adhere the tag pocket to the front cover of the book. Use white acrylic paint (applied to stamp[s] with a cosmetic sponge) to stamp your choice of text on the front cover and along the spine.

10

NINE. Add embellishments.
Adhere embellishments to the cover as desired. For my embellishments, I stamped a sheet of acetate with the name "Susan B. Anthony," using solvent ink. After trimming the acetate to label size, I inserted it into the wire-looped photo holder, then tied a ribbon around the wire. I also added a stamped tab to the pocket.

TEN. Finish cover design. Finish the cover by inserting an old suffragist-related photo or image into the pocket. When finished with the cover, decorate the interior pages with your choice of embellishments.

the inside pages

To complete the book, incorporate ephemera and old photos into the design of the interior pages. I chose decorative paper and embellishments to match the style of the book's cover.

"t for two"
memory page

isn't it funny how something that seems mundane to others can mean so much to you and your loved ones? This cherished photograph is the perfect example. The old tandem bike in the picture may look like a hunk of metal, left to rust in the wicked seasonal weather of the Midwest. But, if this bike could talk, it would share so many fun-filled memories. Just looking at the photo stirs up the stories, like taking the two-wheeled adventure of my life as I rode with my brother-in-law through bumpy irrigation ditches, or riding with my sister and laughing until we could hardly pedal, our normal leg functions hindered by our hysterics. I'm sure you have photos that evoke the same kind of memories—memories that make you say, "Ahhh, those were the days."

1

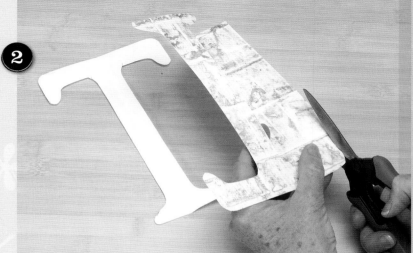

2

ONE. Cover cardstock. Using a paper trimmer, trim a sheet of solid-colored cardstock to 8" × 8" (20cm × 20cm). Cut two sheets of coordinating decorative paper, one to 3" × 8" (8cm × 20cm) and the other to 5" × 8" (13cm × 20cm). Use double-sided tape to adhere each sheet of paper to the cardstock, covering the entire surface.

TWO. Make large letter. Cut out a large letter, measuring 8" (20cm) tall, from decorative paper. (I chose the letter T for "tandem bike," which is the theme of this scrapbook page.) To make the letter, first create and cut out a pattern from a piece of scrap paper; if you are not comfortable drawing the letter freehand, generate it and print it from your computer. Trace the letter onto a piece of decorative paper, then cut out the letter.

MATERIALS

solid-colored cardstock (tan)

decorative paper
* dark burgundy (Diane's Daughter)
* light distressed (Paper Loft)

scrap paper

favorite photograph

rubber stamps
* letters (Hero Arts)

ink (Tsukineko StazOn Black)

embellishments
* lace, about 2" (5cm) wide
* letter stickers (Basic Grey)
* number stickers (EK Success)
* small paper tag, with key clip attached (7 Gypsies)
* several kinds of decorative ribbon (May Arts, Offray)
* decorative brads (Making Memories)
* additional embellishments of your choice, as desired

eyelet

paper trimmer

scissors

Japanese screw punch

eyelet setter and hammer

glue stick

double-sided tape

adhesive dots

pencil

self-healing cutting mat

computer and printer (optional)

3

4

THREE. Add lace trim. Cut a length of lace approximately 8" (20cm) long. Dab glue stick onto the lace and adhere it to the page, placing it vertically about 2½" (6cm) from the left edge.

FOUR. Place photograph. Use double-sided tape to adhere a favorite photograph to the page, placing it to the right of the lace.

FIVE. Add stickers and stamps. Add a few decorative stickers along the bottom edge of the photo. Then, stamp a word or phrase onto a small paper tag.

SIX. Punch hole in letter. With a screw punch, punch a hole somewhere along the top of the paper letter created in step 2. Set the hole with an eyelet, using an eyelet setter and hammer.

5

6

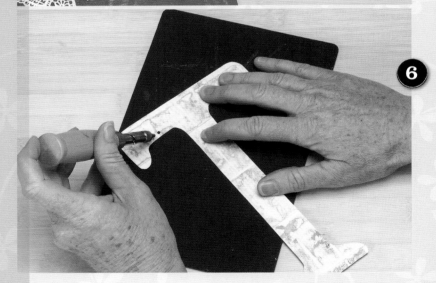

7

8

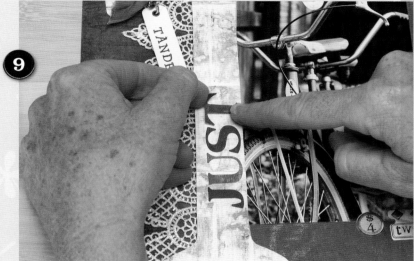

9

SEVEN. **Adhere letter to page.**
Thread a couple lengths of decorative ribbon through the eyelet. Slide the tag from step 5 onto the ribbon, then tie the ribbon in a knot and trim the ends. Adhere the paper letter to the page using double-sided tape, overlapping the photograph. For added security, reinforce the paper to the lace with adhesive dots.

EIGHT. **Add ribbon embellishments.** Create a ribbon embellishment to dress up the right side of the page. To do so, adhere one wide ribbon onto the page, running it over the photograph and around to the reverse side of the page. Add two narrow ribbons on top, securing them with decorative brads. If desired, you can add more brads along the bottom of the photo.

NINE. **Finish page design.** Add your choice of final embellishments to complete the page design. To give this page a finishing touch, I added letter stickers to spell the word "just" over the letter T.

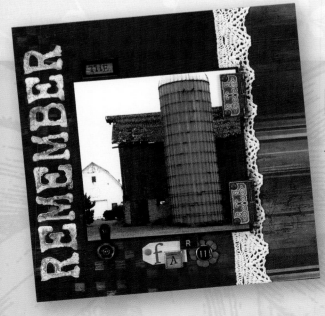

layers
of possibilities

There are all kinds of reasons that we keep certain photographs close to our hearts. I love this particular image simply because it shows the back view of a farm, which most people cannot see from the road. The photo flips open by way of those gorgeous hinges to reveal a bit of hidden journaling. I didn't want to clutter the page with a lot of hardware, so I chose to make the title special by using different elements for the word "farm." To make stamped letters appear faded, like the word "Remember" here, just use diluted acrylic paint.

screen panel
book

taking a walk through the hardware store brings to mind so many fond thoughts of my grandfather. One of my favorite memories comes from the summer that my sisters and I stayed on Grandma and Grandpa's farm, which was equipped with all the basics—a vegetable garden, horses, cows, pigs, chickens and even ducks on the pond. That summer, Grandpa must have visited the hardware store every day. At our young age, we thought he simply needed to buy some tools, but we now realize the importance of the camaraderie and conversation he must have shared with his pals during those visits. I outfitted this little screen book with hardware store finds and photographs that represent Grandpa and his farm.

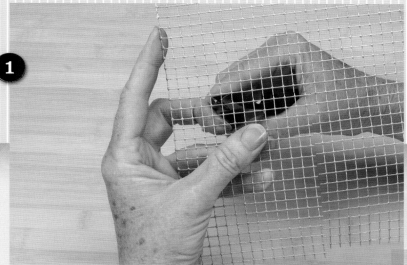

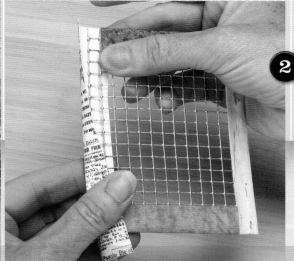

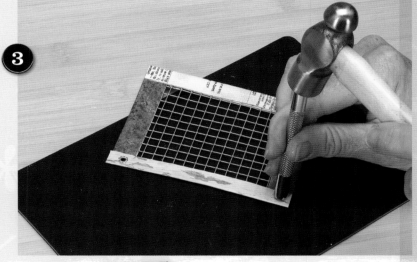

ONE. Cut screen panels. Using wire cutters, cut five 4½" × 3½" (11cm × 9cm) panels of wire screen.

TWO. Cover panel edges. Cut ten 4½" × 1" (11cm × 3cm) strips and ten 3½" × 1" (9cm × 3cm) strips of coordinating decorative paper. (Because these pieces are so small, you can cut the strips from paper scraps or wallpaper samples.) Use the paper strips to cover all four edges of each panel, folding one strip in half over each edge and securing in place with tacky glue.

THREE. Punch holes and set eyelets. Punch two holes through the paper strips on one panel—one in the top left corner and one in the bottom left corner, as shown. Use an eyelet setter and hammer to set an eyelet in each hole. When finished, flip the panel over so that the holes are on the right side. This will be the first (or front) panel of the booklet.

MATERIALS

wire screen

scrap pieces of decorative paper and/or wallpaper samples

ink-jet transparency

favorite photograph(s)

two-part rust kit (Rustoleum)

ribbon (May Arts, Offray)

embellishments
- ✳ miniature metal frames (Magic Scraps)
- ✳ fabric strips
- ✳ suspender clasp
- ✳ decorative brads (Making Memories)
- ✳ other embellishments of your choice, as desired

eyelets

string

scissors

Japanese screw punch

eyelet setter and hammer

tacky glue

double-sided tape

wire cutters

needle-nose pliers

jump rings (optional)

makeup sponges

paper towel

self-healing cutting mat

computer and printer

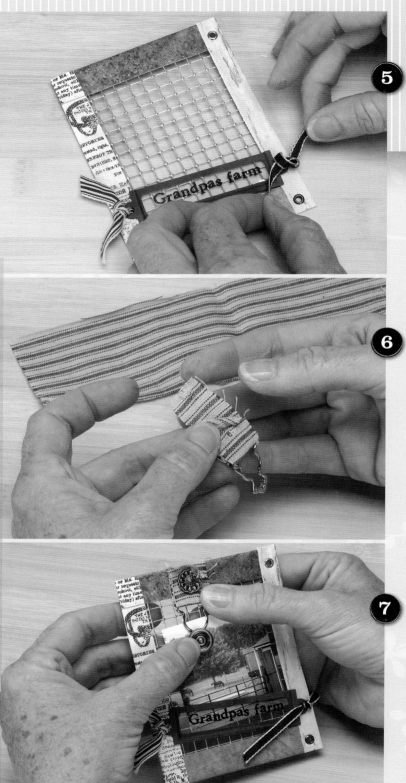

FOUR. Treat miniature frames. Spray the first coat of the two-part rust treatment onto the miniature frame surfaces and let dry. Use a makeup sponge to apply the second coat, then immediately use a dry paper towel to blot off some of the coating; this will give it a naturally-aged look. Allow the frames to dry completely. ✱ NOTE: The two-part rust treatment, which can be found at craft and hardware stores, comes in a kit.

FIVE. Add framed embellishment. To make a text embellishment, create and print text of your choice onto an ink-jet transparency sheet, sizing the word(s) to fit inside the frame. Trim the sheet, then adhere it to the back of the frame with double-sided tape. Place the framed text across the screen panel as desired. Using the frame placement as a reference, punch holes in the paper strips on the left and right sides of the screen panel. Run ribbon through each hole, then slide the frame onto the ribbon. Tie each ribbon in a knot, securing the framed embellishment to the screen panel.

SIX. Create hook embellishment. Tear or cut a piece of fabric into a 3" (8cm) strip. Run about 1" (3cm) of the strip through the suspender hook, then punch or cut a small hole where the fabric overlaps.

SEVEN. Attach photo to panel. Glue the end of the fabric strip to the back of the panel, just below the top edge. Pull the suspender hook over the edge to the front. Locate the holes that you punched through the fabric and punch a corresponding hole through the top paper strip. Set a decorative brad through the holes and fasten. Place a photograph on the panel. Secure the photo to the panel, along with the suspender loop, with another decorative brad.

⑧

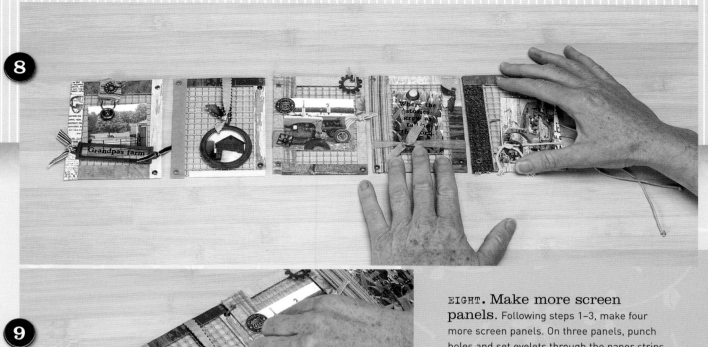

⑨

the inside pages

There's no mistaking the earthy, rural charm of this wire-screen panel book. When I created the interior design, I tried to keep that rustic look consistent through all the panels.

EIGHT. Make more screen panels. Following steps 1–3, make four more screen panels. On three panels, punch holes and set eyelets through the paper strips in each of the four corners. On the last panel, punch two holes—one in the top left corner and one in the bottom left corner. Decorate all four screen panels to coordinate with the first panel, using the paper and embellishments of your choice. When finished, place the panels in a horizontal row, lining up the holes side by side. The first panel should have holes on the right side only, the last panel should have holes on the left side only.

NINE. Attach panels. Attach the screen panels together with ribbon or jump rings, tying one length of ribbon or closing one jump ring through each set of holes, as shown. When all the panels are attached, fold them accordion-style and tie a piece of string around the panels to keep the booklet closed.

carpe diem:

seizing the day

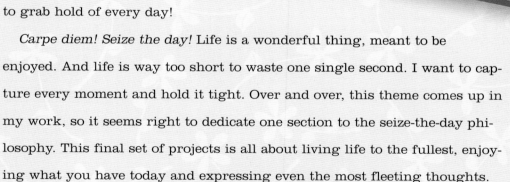

my approach to life has not always been as humorous and fun-loving as it is now. It's funny how age allows us to see things so much more clearly, as our eyesight gets worse! I see the changes in myself as I plod into my midlife years, and this has been something of an awakening experience. The days seem to go increasingly faster with every year that passes. With a new awareness and appreciation of time, I choose to grab hold of every day!

Carpe diem! Seize the day! Life is a wonderful thing, meant to be enjoyed. And life is way too short to waste one single second. I want to capture every moment and hold it tight. Over and over, this theme comes up in my work, so it seems right to dedicate one section to the seize-the-day philosophy. This final set of projects is all about living life to the fullest, enjoying what you have today and expressing even the most fleeting thoughts.

These projects are intended to arouse the spirit of *carpe diem* in different forms. They all make fantastic gift ideas, but don't be surprised if you find that you'd rather keep them (or at least make additional ones) for yourself! I hope you will feel inspired to harness and celebrate your most joyful moments, whether you do it in your own words in a journal or someone else's words in a quote book. Take the time to enjoy life's many layers of joy!

miniature daily
journal

Journaling your thoughts can be a self-healing and rewarding experience. In keeping a journal of positive thoughts, I find that I am able to remember and appreciate the small things that happen to me daily—things that otherwise may be forgotten. This miniature booklet is one example of the many journals I keep in my collection. It is nothing too fancy or intimidating. In fact, its small size and simple design is intentional to encourage a stop-to-smell-the-roses type of journaling. You can slip this journal into your purse or pocket, and then jot down quick observations and brief entries that document the simplest pleasures in life.

1

2

3

ONE. Cover front and back. Using a glue stick, adhere a piece of decorative paper to the front cover of the composition book. Trim any excess paper along the edges and rounded corners of the cover. Cover the back of the book and trim in the same manner, as shown. Distress the edges of the front and back covers with a sanding block.

TWO. Add door knocker. Adhere the door-knocker embellishment to the cover.

THREE. Finish with embellishments. Using tacky glue, adhere a length of decorative ribbon along the spine, then tie a charm onto the knocker with matching ribbon. Finish by adding stamps, rub-on images and other embellishments of your choice to the front cover.

MATERIALS

miniature composition book

decorative paper
❋ cream and white (Scrap-Ease)

rubber stamps
❋ small letters (Hero Arts)
❋ additional designs of your choice, as desired

ink (Tsukineko StazOn Black)

embellishments
❋ adhesive-backed door knocker (EK Success)
❋ ribbon (May Arts, Offray)
❋ charm
❋ rub-on hand image (7 Gypsies)
❋ additional embellishments of your choice, as desired

scissors

glue stick

tacky glue

sanding block

self-healing cutting mat

remember-to-laugh
booklet

i definitely have learned not to sweat the small stuff. It took me awhile, but once I got there, it made life so much easier! I like to send small, encouraging, handmade booklets to my friends, inviting them to adopt this same attitude. Inside these fold-out books the recipients find simple words to help them through their tough times. Words can be a very powerful tool in showing compassion, sharing inspiration or providing solace to those we care about. Just a single word or phrase can make such a difference. I chose the word "laugh" for this booklet. No matter what your chosen words, these tag booklets are the perfect way to convey your message.

1

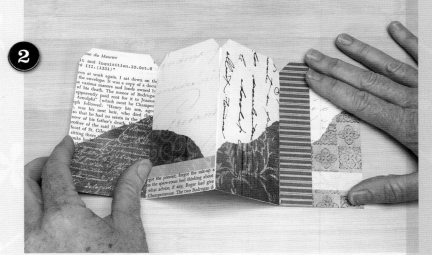

2

ONE. Cover tags. Cut and/or tear four pieces of coordinating decorative paper, one to fit on each panel of the fold-out tag booklet. Use a glue stick to adhere the paper to the panels. Use scissors to trim any excess paper along the edges.

TWO. Add more paper to tags. Cut and tear more pieces of decorative paper into various sizes and shapes. Continue adhering the paper to the panels, layering and overlapping as desired.

MATERIALS

four-panel fold-out tag booklet

decorative papers
✳ light distressed (Basic Grey)
✳ yellow (Daisy D's)
✳ light script (7 Gypsies)
✳ dark script (7 Gypsies)
✳ book text (7 Gypsies)
✳ dark pattern (7 Gypsies)
✳ burgundy (Basic Grey)
✳ stripes (Daisy D's)
✳ green tiles (EK Success)

chipboard

rubber stamps
✳ letters (My Sentiments Exactly)
✳ additional designs of your choice, as desired

ink (Tsukineko StazOn Black, Ranger Distress Ink)

embellishments
✳ charms (I kan'dee)
✳ decorative brads (Making Memories)
✳ ribbons (May Arts, Offray)
✳ embellishments of your choice, as desired

paper trimmer

scissors

Japanese screw punch

glue stick

tacky glue

pencil

self-healing cutting mat

3

4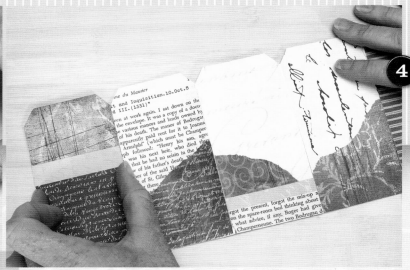

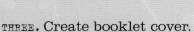

5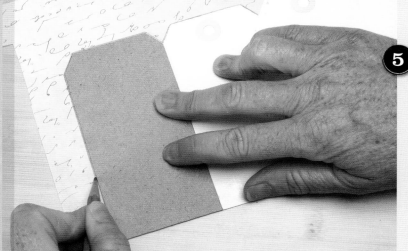

6

THREE. Create booklet cover.
Fold up the tag booklet. Using the booklet as a template, trace a tag shape onto a piece of chipboard. Cut out the tag shape to create a sturdy cover for the booklet. Cover the bottom two-thirds of the chipboard tag with decorative paper, adhering it with a glue stick and trimming any excess paper along the edges.

FOUR. Finish cover. Finish covering the chipboard tag, adhering two more strips of decorative paper to cover the top third. Unfold the booklet, then place the chipboard tag in the proper position for the cover by butting it against the far left panel, as shown.

FIVE. Create hinge paper. Holding them together, flip the chipboard cover and the booklet onto a sheet of decorative paper. Again, butt the chipboard tag against the end tag, aligning the bottom edges. Use a pencil to trace around the two tags, as shown.

SIX. Add hinge paper to panels. Cut the hinge pattern out of the decorative paper, trimming along the pencil lines. With the cover and booklet still face down, realign the cover panel with the end panel. Use a glue stick to adhere the hinge paper to these two panels. This will join the two tags, creating a single unit.

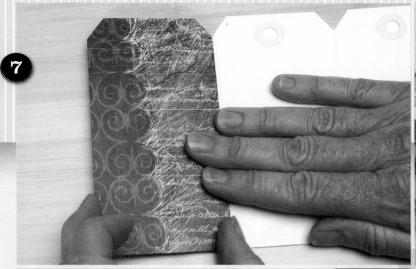

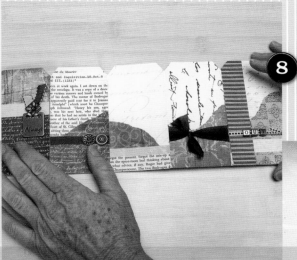

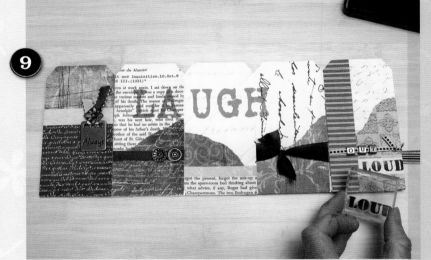

SEVEN. Cover end tag. Cut and cover another chipboard tag, as you did in step 3. With the booklet still face down, run a glue stick over the surface of the far left tag. Place the chipboard tag, decorated side up, on top of the tag, making sure the edges line up perfectly. Use your hand to burnish the two surfaces together.

EIGHT. Add embellishments. Flip the tag booklet back over and place it face up on your work surface. Add your choice of embellishments, such as charms and decorative brads, onto each tag panel, using a screw punch and/or tacky glue as necessary. Run different decorative ribbons around each tag, and secure them in place by gluing the ends of the ribbon onto the backs of the tags.

NINE. Add text. Create the text of your choice across the tags, using stamps and scrapbook embellishments. Your text booklet can now be folded or displayed accordion-style.

layers of possibilities

I love the phrase "Let what you love be what you do," perhaps because I identify with the connection between strong emotion and an important life choice. If you have a favorite phrase, incorporate it into a variation project like this one, in which I spread the phrase out over four tags. Finish the look by adding a few decorative touches with stamps and ribbons.

layers

113

bound quote
collection

i love incorporating quotes, or "words to live by," into my projects. Some quotes are full of wisdom, offering insights to help you understand the world. Others are just plain funny, eliciting a good chuckle or two. It always amazes me how just a few words—wise, silly or somewhere in between—can provide such great stress relief. One of my favorite sources for quotes is baseball legend Yogi Berra. His "Yogi-isms" are humorous, and often a little confusing, too! My very favorite quotes in life are those inspirational reminders to "seize the day." I made this little hinged booklet to hold a selection of carpe diem-themed quotes.

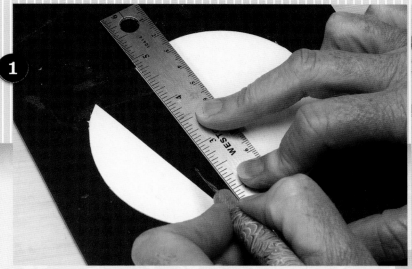

ONE. Create front cover. Measure in about 1" (3cm) from the edge of one disc. Place a ruler across the coaster at this 1" (3cm) point, as shown. Holding the ruler in place, run a craft knife along the edge of the ruler, cutting the disc into two panels.

TWO. Line discs with paper. Using a glue stick, cover one side (or both sides) of the uncut disc with decorative paper. Then cover both sides of the larger panel from step 1 with the same decorative paper. Cover one side of the smaller panel with different decorative paper. Trim any excess paper off the edges of all the disc components.

THREE. Make interior pages. Place the uncut disc on a sheet of decorative paper, then trace the shape onto the paper eight or nine times. Cut out each circle to create pages for the book.

MATERIALS

two chipboard discs (River City Rubber Works)

decorative paper
* purples (Paper Pizazz)
* floral (Colors By Design)
* green crackle (K&Company)

rubber stamps
* small letters (Hero Arts)
* large letters (My Sentiments Exactly)
* additional designs of your choice, as desired

ink (Tsukineko StazOn Black, Ranger Distress Inks)

small metal hinges (Making Memories)

brads (Lasting Impressions)

ribbon (Yarn Market, Offray)

embellishments
* small paper tags (Hero Arts)
* small jump ring
* additional embellishments of your choice, as desired

craft knife

scissors

Japanese screw punch

glue stick

tacky glue

double-sided tape (optional)

sanding block

ruler

pencil

self-healing cutting mat

computer and printer, or pen (or both)

FOUR. Punch hinge holes.
Place the cut panels from step 1 together to re-form a circle. Position two small metal hinges over the two panels, aligning the center of the hinges with the cut line. Use a pencil to mark the placement of the hinge holes on each panel. Use a screw punch to punch each panel where marked.

FIVE. Punch holes in back cover. Place the smaller punched panel on top of the back cover, aligning the edges. Punch corresponding holes in the back cover.

SIX. Punch pages. Stack two or three of the interior pages created in step 3. Place the smaller punched panel on top of the stack, aligning the edges. Punch corresponding holes through the pages. Repeat with the remaining interior pages.

SEVEN. Attach hinges to front cover. Secure the hinges to the larger panel of the front cover, adhering the hinges to the cover with tacky glue. Then, use brads to secure the hinges in place.

EIGHT. Add pages and back cover. Secure the hinges to the smaller panel of the front cover, adhering the hinges with tacky glue to complete the front cover. Run one brad through each hole of the hinge, then slide the interior pages and the back cover (paper-covered side facing out) through the prongs of the brad. Bend the prongs flush with the back cover, securing all the book components together.

9

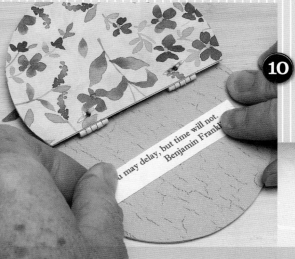

10

11

NINE. Embellish cover. Distress the front and back covers by running the edges along the surface of a sanding block. Then use your choice of embellishments to add the desired text to the front cover. I used stamps, stickers and tags to spell out "Quotes 2 Live By."

TEN. Add quotes. Print out some of your favorite inspirational quotes on your computer, then cut them out. Adhere them to the interior pages with glue or double-sided tape. Or, if you'd rather, handwrite the quotes directly on the pages.

ELEVEN. Add ribbon. Punch a hole through the bottom center of the front cover, interior pages and back cover. Run a length of ribbon through all the holes, then secure the book shut by tying the ribbon in a knot. For a little extra embellishment, run a jump ring through the hole on the front cover, then close the ring securely; run the ribbon through the back cover, the interior pages and the jump ring, tying the ribbon in a knot to keep the book shut.

favorite quotes

Below I have listed some of my favorite "Seize the Day" quotes. I love to weave these into my projects whenever I can.

And in the end, it's not the years in your life that count.
It's the life in your years. | ABRAHAM LINCOLN

Spend the afternoon. You can't take it with you. | ANNIE DILLARD

I still find each day too short for all the thoughts I want to think,
all the walks I want to take, all the books I want to read and
all the friends I want to see. | JOHN BURROUGHS

Men for the sake of getting a living forget to live. | MARGARET FULLER

You will never find time for anything. If you want time
you must make it. | CHARLES BUXTON

You live longer once you realize that any time
spent being unhappy is wasted. | RUTH E. RENKL

You may delay, but time will not. | BENJAMIN FRANKLIN

When you were born, you cried and the world rejoiced. Live your life in such a
manner that when you die the world cries and you rejoice. | INDIAN SAYING

collective thoughts
journal

a couple years ago, my mother gave me the journal that my grandmother had kept during her teenage years. After reading a few entries, I realized what a hard life Grandma had had as a young girl. Little did Mom know what a gift this was. The journal has become quite an inspiration for me, right down to my soul. Today, thanks to this special keepsake, I am very committed to keeping a journal myself. I hope that my own grandchildren will read my journal of collective thoughts someday, and that they will discover and share my appreciation for life.

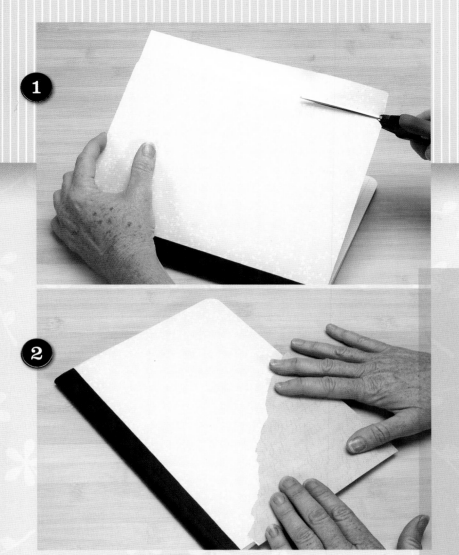

ONE. Apply paper to book covers. Use a glue stick to adhere a sheet of decorative paper to the front cover of a composition book, covering the entire surface. Trim any excess paper along the edges of the cover. Cover the back cover with decorative papers in the same manner.

TWO. Add layer of torn paper. Tear a piece of different decorative paper diagonally, leaving a triangular shape. Adhere the torn paper to the front cover with a glue stick, covering the lower right corner. Trim any excess paper along the edges of the cover.

MATERIALS

composition book

decorative paper
* blue (Daisy D's)
* beige (Chatterbox)
* beige leaves (Lasting Impressions)

vellum

rubber stamps
* small letters (Hero Arts)
* large letters (My Sentiments Exactly)
* flowers (Hero Arts)
* additional designs of your choice, as desired

ink (Ranger Distress Ink)

embellishments
* paper tabs (7 Gypsies)
* letter stickers (Marcella by Kay)
* lace trim
* buttons
* square conchos (Scrap Works)
* round paper tag (Autumn Leaves)
* flower embellishment (Prima)
* ribbon
* brads
* studs (Scrap Works)
* additional embellishments of your choice, as desired

elastic or twill tape

thread

pen

paper trimmer

scissors

awl

heavy needle

glue stick

tacky glue

double-sided tape

self-healing cutting mat

sewing machine (optional)

THREE. Add vellum pocket. Cut a piece of vellum into a 5" × 7" (13cm × 18cm) rectangle. Tear off the upper left corner in a diagonal direction. Center the torn vellum on the cover, then use double-sided tape to tack down the vellum along the left, right and bottom edges. ✱ NOTE: Glue makes vellum buckle, so always use double-sided tape to adhere vellum to a surface.

FOUR. Add paper along spine. Cut a strip of coordinating paper to the length of the spine. Adhere the strip along the spine with a glue stick, and trim off any excess paper along the top and bottom edges of the book. Adhere two paper tabs to the lower right edge of the vellum, for text to be added later.

FIVE. Add title. Add a journal title to the cover design as desired, using letter stickers and rubber stamps to spell words along the spine and along the top.

SIX. Add lace trim. Cut a length of lace to the width of the vellum pocket. Use double-sided tape or glue to adhere the lace along the bottom edge of the pocket. Adhere another length of lace along the edge of the spine, and trim off any excess lace along the top and bottom edges of the cover.

SEVEN. Attach loop to cover. Cut a 2" (5cm) length of elastic or twill tape. Fold the elastic in half, then use double-sided tape to overlap the two ends and secure, to the right edge of the vellum pocket, as shown. This loop will become the pen holder.

layers

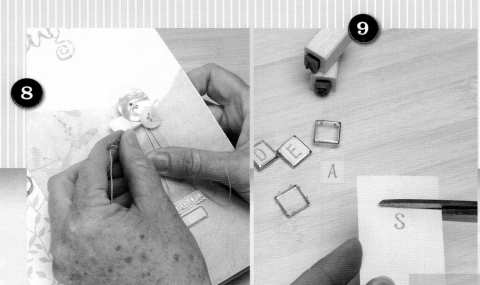

EIGHT. Stitch loop to cover. Stitch a couple of decorative buttons to the cover, running the stitches through the ends of the elastic to keep the loop securely in place. Do not allow the buttons to obscure the loop, as it must be able to hold a pen. ✱ **NOTE:** After determining where you will place the buttons, you may find it helpful to pre-pierce holes through the cover with an awl.

NINE. Make text embellishments. Create text embellishments, using words and phrases related to creativity and artistic inspiration. First, stamp the letters onto paper, then trim the paper and slide each letter into a square concho.

TEN. Add text embellishments. Using tacky glue, adhere the text embellishments created from step 9 to the cover. Add more creativity-themed embellishments of your choice, such as a stamped decorative tag.

ELEVEN. Create notecard tag for pocket. Create a decorative notecard tag to fit into the vellum pocket, then stamp and embellish as desired. When finished, you can leave the tag blank, as shown, or write a personalized message on it. Insert the tag into the pocket. Finish the cover design with stamps, ribbons, brads and studs of your choice. Complete the journal by inserting a pen into the pen-holder loop.

TIP

You can also use machine stitching as a way of adding extra embellishment. Straight or zigzag stitching not only secures the paper to the surface, but it also adds extra flair!

celebration
wine box

i just can't seem to leave things alone. One way or another, I must always mark my territory with a special design, a sentimental creation or a personal touch. It should come as no surprise, then, that I love to alter anything I can get my hands on. For example, I recently purchased a simple wine box from a store, and I couldn't wait to bring it home and transform it into a decorative piece. I was attracted to this particular box because it boasted an unusual shape and some unique hardware attachments. If you are unable to find a similar box, don't worry—any wine box will do. Wine suggests a spirit of celebration, which is perfect for the theme of carpe diem. To life!

1

2

ONE. Cover box with paper.
Remove the hardware (if any) from the wine box. Using a glue stick or tacky glue, cover the surface of the wine box and lid with a base layer of decorative paper.

TWO. Prepare paper for collage.
Cut or tear pieces of coordinating decorative paper to collage over the wine box. If desired, you can distress the paper pieces and further embellish them with stamped designs.

MATERIALS

wine box

decorative paper
* blues (Basic Grey)
* beige script (7 Gypsies)
* newspaper (7 Gypsies)
* light brown stripes (Daisy D's)
* light script (K&Company)
* small script (Autumn Leaves)

rubber stamps
* letters
* flowers (Hero Arts)
* additional designs of your choice, as desired

ink (Ranger Distress Ink)

embellishments
* ruler sticker (EK Success)
* typewriter key stickers (EK Success)
* rivet stickers (EK Success)
* game letter tiles (EK Success)
* metal tab (7 Gypsies)
* key (K&Company)
* circle charm (I kan'dee)

* flowers (Prima)
* ribbon (Offray)
* fibers (Basic Grey, Yarn Market)
* plastic brads (Chatterbox)
* jewelry tags

paper trimmer

craft knife

scissors

glue stick

tacky glue

double-sided tape

plastic card for burnishing (such as a credit card, hotel key card, etc.)

label maker (Dymo)

screwdriver

self-healing cutting mat

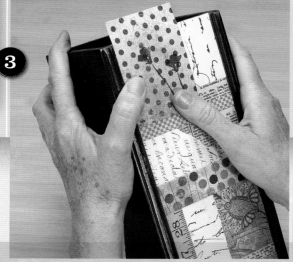

3

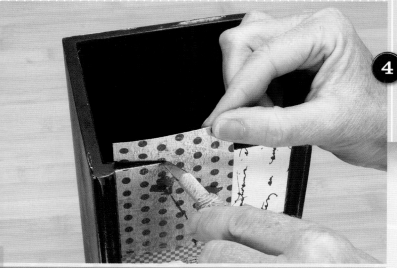

4

5

THREE. **Collage paper onto box.**
Cover the front surface of the box with the
pieces of decorative paper prepared in step 2.
Cut, tear or trim the paper, then use a glue
stick to adhere the paper to the box in layers
until you achieve a design that you like. Use a
plastic card to burnish the pieces in place.

FOUR. **Trim paper.** Trim any excess
paper with a craft knife, running the blade
along the edges of the box.

FIVE. **Cover lid and back of
box.** Cover the surface of the lid with layers of decorative paper, continuing the design
created on the front of the box. Finish the box
by adhering layers of decorative paper to the
back of the box.

SIX. **Add embellishments.** Decide
on a carpe diem-themed message to display
on the wine box. (I chose "Live life to the fullest.") Plan out how you will arrange the words
on the front of the box, then add a few of
the words to the box, using
stickers, the label maker
and stamps.

6

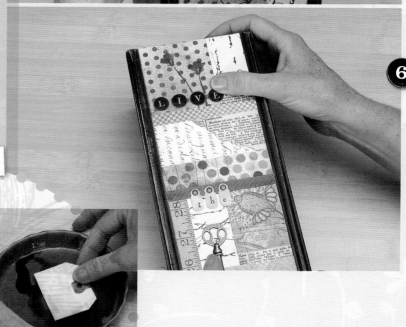

T I P

When preparing
my decorative
paper to collage onto
the surface of the wine
box and lid, I stained
some of the paper with
a coffee solution. See
page 13 for a descrip-
tion of this technique.

layers

7

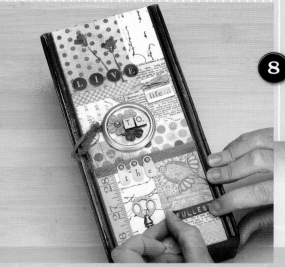

8

9

SEVEN. Make embellishments.
Use a variety of tags, handmade labels, stickers, stamps, ribbons, fibers and more to create decorative embellishments for the box. Among these embellishments, include labels and tags that feature the remaining words from your message.

EIGHT. Add final embellishments. Add the embellishments from step 7 to the surface of the box and lid, securing them in place with double-sided tape or glue. Arrange the text embellishments on the box as desired to complete the message started in step 6.

NINE. Reassemble box. When finished embellishing the box and lid, reassemble the wine box and secure the original hardware back in place.

layers of possibilities

Have you ever had a day so perfect that you wanted it to last forever? Take note of those days, and "house" them within a project for memory's sake. After keeping this cigar box for ages, I decided to use it for just such a project. I covered the lid with torn paper, mixing script and patterns. Then, I added the title in a montage fashion, using tags, stamps, game pieces and more. If you have an interesting box or container stashed away somewhere, there's no time like the present to transform it into something amazing!

resources

I live in a remote area with a very limited selection of art and craft stores in close proximity, so I have learned to find my needs elsewhere. With its endless selection of products and ideas, the Internet has been an excellent source for tools and materials. The downfall, however, is the lack of opportunity to feel and touch the items for sale. Nothing beats a well-stocked store, which invites you to let your fingers do the shopping. For this reason, I encourage you to explore and support your local art, craft and fabric stores whenever possible.

paper

American Traditional Designs
(800) 448-6656
www.americantraditional.com

Anna Griffin
(888) 817-8170
www.annagriffin.com

Autumn Leaves
(800) 588-6707
www.autumnleaves.com

Basic Grey
(801) 544-1116
www.basicgrey.com

Bazzill Basics
(480) 558-8557
www.bazzillbasics.com

Chatterbox
(888) 416-6260
www.chatterboxinc.com

Colormates
(888) 843-6455
www.worldwinpapers.com

Colors by Design
(800) 832-8436
www.colorsbydesign.com

Creative Imaginations
(800) 942-6487
www.cigift.com

Daisy D's
(888) 601-8955
www.daisydspaper.com

Diane's Daughters
(800) 692-3566
www.dianesdaughters.com

Grafix
(800) 447-2349
www.grafixarts.com

Karen Foster Designs
(801) 451-9779
www.karenfosterdesign.com

Lasting Impressions
(800) 936-2677
www.lastingimpressions.com

Me and My Big Ideas
www.meandmybigideas.com

Magic Scraps
(904) 482-0092
www.magicscraps.com

The Paper Company
(973) 406-5000
www.anwcrestwood.com

Paper Loft
(801) 254-1961
www.paperloft.com

**Paper Pizazz
(by Hot Off The Press)**
(888) 300-3406
www.paperwishes.com

Scrap-Ease
(480) 830-4581
www.scrap-ease.com

adhesives

Aleene's
(800) 438-6226
www.duncancrafts.com

Plaid
(800) 842-4197
www.plaidonline.com

Glue Dots
www.gluedots.com

Duck Products
(800) 321-0253
www.duckproducts.com

embellishments

ARTchix Studio
(250) 478-5985
www.artchixstudio.com

I kan'dee
(801) 235-1520
www.pebblesinc.com

Limited Edition
(800) 229-1019
www.limitededitionrs.com

Prima Flowers
(909) 627-5532
www.mulberrypaperflowers.com

Scrap Works
(801) 363-1010
www.scrapworks.com

inks and paints

Folk Art
(800) 842-4197
www.plaidonline.com

Krylon
www.krylon.com

Ranger
(732) 389-3535
www.rangerink.com

Rustoleum
(800) 553-8444
www.rustoleum.com

Tsukineko
(425) 883-7733
www.tsukineko.com

miscellaneous scrapbooking

7 Gypsies
(877) 749-7797
www.7gypsies.com

Design Originals
(800) 877-7820
www.d-originals.com

EK Success
www.eksuccess.com

K&Company
(888) 244-2083
www.kandcompany.com

Making Memories
(801) 294-0430
www.makingmemories.com

River City Rubber Works
(877) 735-2276
www.rivercityrubberworks.com

notions and ribbons

Dritz
www.dritz.com

The Leather Factory
(800) 433-3201
www.leatherfactory.com

May Arts
www.mayarts.com

Offray
www.offray.com

Yarn Market
(888) 996-9276
www.yarnmarket.com

rubber stamps

Hero Arts
(800) 822-4376
www.heroarts.com

JustRite Stampers
(847) 808-7345
www.productperformers.com

My Sentiments Exactly
(719) 260-6001
www.sentiments.com

tools

3M
(888) 364-3577
www.3m.com

DYMO
(800) 426-7827
www.dymo.com

Fiskars
(866) 348-5661
www.fiskars.com

index

acetate, 8-9, 29, 37, 73-75, 93, 97
adhesives, 8-9
awls, 11

board book, 95-97
book knob, 57, 60
box pattern, 61
boxes, 8, 57-61
brads, 10, 29
burnishing, 58-59, 74, 81-82, 123-124
buttons, 24-25, 121

canvas, 49-51
cardstock, 8-9, 81
chalkboard paint, 27
charms, 10, 77, 109, 123, 125
chipboard, 8, 27-28, 57-60
    discs, 23-25, 115-117
    letters, 10
    tags, 33, 112-113
cigar box, 125
clipboard, 68-71
coasters, 30-33
collage, 90-93
compact disc pocket folders, 81-85
composition book, 109, 119-121
conchos, 119, 121
craft knives, 10-12
crochet thread, 53-55
cutting mat, 11-12

découpage medium, 8-9, 49-50
distressing, 9, 13, 123
door knocker, 108-109
doorknobs, 10, 36

electrical outlet plates, 76-79
embellishments, 9-10
embossing, 9, 67
eyelets, 10-11, 15

fabric, 84-85, 104-105
flowers, 10, 32, 73, 75
foam dots, 9
frames, 10, 41-43, 91, 103-105

game letters, 25, 28, 31, 33, 123, 125
glues, 8-9

hinges, 65-67, 82, 101, 112, 115-117
hole-punching, 15, 36

images, 70, 109
    See also photographs, vintage
inks, 8-9, 13, 69-70, 74

Japanese screw punch, 11, 15
jump rings, 105, 115, 117

keys, 35, 37, 123-125

label holder, 51
label maker, 81, 84, 123-125
label staples, 65-66
lace, 10, 99-101, 120
letters, 10, 21, 28, 91-93
    faded, 101
    large, 99-101
    stamped, 115, 117, 119-121
    sticker, 10, 21, 91, 117, 119-120, 123-125
    See also game letters; words
library pockets, 45-47, 90-93
lid, box, 57-61

matchboxes, 57, 59-60
materials, 8-11
    See also specific material
metal clips, 19
montage, 125
movement, collapsible, 59

office supplies, 9-10, 87, 90
    See also library pockets

paints, 9, 27, 50, 83
paper, 8-9, 12, 67
    decorative, 8-9, 35, 123-125
paper bags, 52-55
paper trimmer, 10-12, 69
patterns, box and lid, 61
pen holder, 120-121
photo holder, 95-97
photographs, vintage, 88-105
pockets, 36, 45-47, 90-93, 120

quotes, 114, 116-117

ribbons, 10, 21, 42-43, 55, 79, 101-105, 117
rubber stamps, 8-10, 14, 50, 84
rust kit, 103-104

sanding, 11, 13, 95
scissors, 10-12
scoring, 11, 74
sewing notions, 10
slide mounts, 27-29, 73-75, 91-93
snaps, 95-96
sponges, 11
staining, 9, 13
stamping, 8-9, 14, 37, 74, 84, 93
stencils, letter, 10

stickers, 9, 35, 99-101
    letter, 10, 21, 91, 117, 123-125
stitching, 11, 46, 121
suspender hook, 104-105

tabs, 77-78, 82, 95, 97, 119-121, 123
tag booklet, 47, 110-113
tags, 9-10, 115, 117, 119, 121
    chipboard, 33
    decorative, 73, 75, 83-84
    drycleaner, 24
    notecard, 121
    paper, 28, 31-32, 45-47, 65, 83, 96
tape, 9, 36
    gaffing, 65
title labels, 84
tools, 8-11
transparencies, 8, 49-51, 69-71

vellum, 8-9, 36, 120
vintage materials, 9-10, 87-105

windows, 78
wire screen, 102-105
wood discs, 49-50
words
    from books, 31-33, 83
    computer-generated, 54, 99
    cutout, 30-33
    stamped, 9, 14
    on stickers, 35-37
    See also game letters; letters

Check out these other
North Light titles
for more great ideas!

The Artful Card
Alison Eads

The Artful Card showcases over 25 gorgeous cards and keepsakes made with collage techniques using printed papers, embellishments and found objects. With her unique, romantic style and simple yet clever techniques, Alison Eads brings the hottest trends in scrapbooking to the card-making world. Whether you're making a romantic card for your someone special, or you just want to send a friend or family member a handmade message to show you care, you're sure to find just the right thing inside *The Artful Card.*

ISBN-10: 1-58180-680-9
ISBN-13: 978-1-58180-680-9
paperback 128 pages 33269

Collage Discovery Workshop
Claudine Hellmuth

A medley of ideas, techniques and lessons on being an artist, *Collage Discovery Workshop* is the perfect medium to help you unleash your creative potential. Discover innovative techniques and demonstrations specifically designed to achieve the eclectic collage effect that has become so popular today. Claudine Hellmuth will introduce you to the basics of collage, show you different image-transferring techniques and lead you through a series of creative exercises that are sure to ignite the creative spark in every crafter!

ISBN-10: 1-58180-343-5
ISBN-13: 978-1-58180-343-3
paperback 128 pages 32313

Texture Effects for Rubber Stamping
Nancy Curry

Crafters can satisfy their craving for texture with this treasure trove of 37 elegant card and gift projects. Inside, you'll find an abundance of texture-making techniques, including stamping with metallic paints, resist effects, alcohol inks, layers of acetate, watercolors and embellishments. Even better, this book is about more than just cards—there are also fresh ideas for turning ordinary boxes, tags, clocks and tiles into memorable gift items. *Texture Effects for Rubber Stamping* is an inspirational resource that crafters will turn to time after time for ideas and instruction.

ISBN-10: 1-58180-558-6
ISBN-13: 978-1-58180-558-1
paperback 128 pages 33014

Artful Memories
Carol Wingert and Tena Sprenger

Renowned scrapbook designers Carol Wingert and Tena Sprenger share their distictive style and gorgeous artistry in 20 step-by-step projects to capture your most treasured memories. From adorable mini-books to framed quotes, you'll learn tricks of the trade from the cream of the crop, using paper, fabric, board books, decorative fibers and more! Express yourself uniquely as you capture your fondest memories artisically, and create your own *Artful Memories* today.

ISBN-10: 1-58180-810-0
ISBN-13: 978-158180-810-0
paperback 128 pages 33488

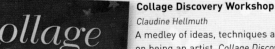

THESE AND OTHER FINE NORTH LIGHT TITLES ARE AVAILABLE FROM YOUR LOCAL ART AND CRAFT RETAILER, BOOKSTORE OR ONLINE SUPPLIER.